HOLY BIBLE

GOD BEHAVIN BADLY

Is the God of the Old Testament
Angry, Sexist and Racist?

DAVID T. LAMB

"This is a book which not only should be read by those [who are] into apologetics, but read by all Christians in our churches. It is striking right at the heart of one of the most pressing questions being asked today and we cannot ignore this. *God Behaving Badly* is an extremely helpful book in wrestling with these very difficult questions in a winsome, biblical and readable way. If you are at all missionally living in our culture and aware of the questions being asked and challenges to Christianity, then you really cannot help but read this book!"

DAN KIMBALL, author of *They Like Jesus but Not the Church*

"Dave Lamb's book is a popular apologetic that answers the question, 'Is the God of the Old Testament angry, sexist and racist?' He prefaces his answers with a solid biblical interpretation guideline. The author emphatically states, 'When we approach Scripture, we must take the context seriously.' Dave really does that! The word *context* appears 59 times, scattered throughout the book. Dave's solid contextual analysis of passages—which might appear to say, Yes, Yes, Yes in answer to the question about God's anger, his view of gender and his view of races—was a highlight for me. Dave's unraveling of many problematic texts in terms of contextual analysis is superb. In addition, his many, many masterful word studies shed light on his contextual analyses. Dave writes with winsome humor. He loves the Old Testament, and you can tell that as you read the popularly written, academically sound, easy to read flow of material in each chapter. After reading Dave's book, I am sure you will appreciate that Dave views the God of the Old Testament and the God of the New Testament as one."

BOBBY CLINTON, professor of leadership, School of Intercultural Studies at Fuller Theological Seminary

"It has been said that if you love something long enough it reveals itself to you—that love is a hermeneutical key to unlocking the mysteries of life itself. This is especially true for the Bible and the God of the Bible, for God is love and can only be truly known in love. David Lamb has loved his way into understanding Yahweh more fully; subsequently he can lovingly help us to 'see' and experience God in new and revealing ways."

ALAN HIRSCH, author of *The Forgotten Ways*

"In many of our African American churches we frequently recite the refrain 'God is good all the time and all the time God is good.' *God Behaving Badly* is an engaging, thoughtful, witty and helpful book that can give all of us Christian readers a bit more confidence when reciting that refrain. David Lamb gives sound guidance for understanding a difficult topic. Lamb offers an apologetic for not only believing in God but also believing that God is good—even as he is portrayed in the Old Testament. Professor Lamb's scholarship is sound, and his sense of humor had me laughing out loud. Not many theology books can do that! I'm going to use this book in class and enthusiastically recommend it to my congregants!"

REV. DENNIS R. EDWARDS, Ph.D., pastor, Peace Fellowship Church, Washington, D.C.

"Let's face it: God gets a lot of bad press—it can be a little embarrassing. So even the title of Dave Lamb's book gave me hope. Dave gives honest voice and deliberate attention to some of the most troublesome questions humans have ever asked, and brings not only answers but develops our view of God too. The most thrilling thing about this book is that I can recommend it to both the faithful and the skittish, to friends and students and people who think about God and aren't sure what to think."

ALISON SIEWERT, New Ministry Developer, Presbyterian Church (U.S.A.), and editor, *Worship Team Handbook*

"I will require my college students to read this book. I became sensitive to the 'God questions' in the Bible because students asked me questions that came straight from troubled hearts. This book is written for students and speaks with wit and wisdom to the questions they have."

SCOT MCKNIGHT, Karl A. Olsson Professor in Religious Studies, North Park University

"David Lamb faces up to all the questions that most often trouble people about the God of the Old Testament. Written in a winsome and engaging way, this book is going to help many who wonder if the God of the Old Testament is indeed the God and Father of our Lord Jesus Christ."

JOHN GOLDINGAY, David Allan Hubbard Professor of Old Testament, Fuller Theological Seminary

Is the God of the Old Testament
Angry, Scxist and Racist?

David T. Lamb

IVP Books

An imprint of InterVarsity Press
Downers Grove, Illinois

InterVarsity Press
P.O. Box 1400, Downers Grove, IL 60515-1426
ivpress.com
email@ivpress.com

InterVarsity Press® is the book-publishing division of InterVarsity Christian Fellowship/USA®, a movement of students and faculty active on campus at hundreds of universities, colleges and schools of nursing in the United States of America, and a member movement of the International Fellowship of Evangelical Students. For information about local and regional activities, visit intervarsity.org.

Scripture quotations, unless otherwise noted, are from The Holy Bible, English Standard Version, copyright © 2001 by Crossway Bibles, a division of Good News Publishers. Used by permission. All rights reserved.

Published in association with the literary agency of Daniel Literary Group, Nashville, TN

Cover design: Cindy Kiple
Interior design: Beth Hagenberg
Images: Bible: Margaret Edwards/iStockphoto
        crushed white paper: Duncan Babbage/iStockphoto
        masking tape: loops7/iStockphoto

ISBN 978-0-8308-3826-4

Printed in the United States of America ∞

Library of Congress Cataloging-in-Publication Data

Lamb, David T. (David Trout), 1962-
  God behaving badly: is the God of the Old Testament angry, sexist,
  and racist? / David T. Lamb.
      p. cm.
  Includes bibliographical references (p.   ) and index.
  ISBN 978-0-8308-3826-4 (pbk.: alk. paper)
  1. God—Biblical teaching. 2. Bible. O.T.—Theology. 3.
Apologetics. I. Title.
  BS1192.6.L35 2011
  230'.0411—dc22

                                                          2010052971

P   21   20   19   18   17   16   15   14   13   12   11

Y   26   25   24   23   22   21   20   19   18   17

To Shannon,

my partner, my friend,

my soul mate.

CONTENTS

1

A BAD REPUTATION

How does one reconcile the loving God of the Old Testament with the harsh God of the New Testament?

When I ask this question of students, at first they are shocked, and then most assume that I have simply misspoken, as I am prone to do. They typically have heard the question inverted, along these lines: "How did the mean Old Testament God morph into a nice guy like Jesus?" I assure them that this time, at least, I have not accidentally inverted my words. I then observe that God in the Old Testament is consistently described as slow to anger and abounding in steadfast love,[1] but Jesus speaks about hell more than anyone else in Scripture.[2] The word *hell* doesn't even show up in English translations of the Old Testament.

My question usually provokes a lively discussion. Eventually I assure the class that I believe that the God of both the Old and the New Testaments can be characterized by love. This book is my attempt to reconcile the supposedly contradictory portrayals of God in the two testaments, but first let me explain how I ended up teaching about the loving God of the Old Testament.

More than ten years ago, I had to decide whether to focus on the Old Testament or the New Testament for study and teaching. It was one of the most important decisions of my life. I love the whole Bible, and it was painful to think about just focusing on one section of it. I thought perhaps I should select the New Testament, because my favorite book was Mark's Gospel, and I had spent more time teaching it than any other section of Scripture. But then I hesitated because the world of New Testament studies seemed crowded. Finding an available New Testament research topic felt like looking for a parking space in the Target lot on Christmas Eve (not that I would have any personal experience of that). It would have been difficult for me to come up with fresh ideas that weren't heretical.

So I considered the Old Testament. If I focused on the Old Testament, I wouldn't have to worry about bumping into someone else working on the same obscure half-verse. I also didn't need to be quite so paranoid about heresy, because we expect to find weird stuff in the Old Testament.

But the most compelling factor drawing me toward studying the Old Testament was God himself. The God of the Old Testament was fascinating to me. He became really angry, but was also extraordinarily patient. He seemed to view women and wives as property, but he also selected women as spiritual and political leaders over the nation of Israel. He commanded Israel to vanquish the Canaanites, but also to care for the poor, the widows, the orphans and the foreigners. God in the Old Testament was complex. There was so much about God in the Old Testament that I didn't understand. I thought I could study the Old Testament for the rest of my life and never feel bored.

I chose the Old Testament.

A decade later I still can't imagine getting tired of studying the Old Testament. Nothing gives me more joy than teaching it. (Well, almost nothing.) I love the Old Testament, and in particular examining the God who is revealed there.

Over the years, though, I have noticed that atheists, agnostics and even Christians perceive the God of the Old Testament negatively. They read the same passages I have just mentioned and instead of seeing a complex portrayal of God that requires more study, they focus on the problematic aspects. As a result, they often ask about reconciling the harsh God of the Old Testament with the loving God of the New Testament. To them he seems angry, sexist and racist.

The God of the Old Testament has a bad reputation.

Is the God of the Old Testament Really Angry, Sexist and Racist?

If you have spent time reading the Old Testament, you probably know what I'm talking about. While reading about the ark of the covenant's procession to Jerusalem, how many of us have wondered what Uzzah did that was so bad? Did God really have to instantly smite him for simply preventing the ark from tipping over (2 Sam 6:7)? Shouldn't Uzzah have been rewarded? Why was God so mad at him? Is the God of the Old Testament always angry?

After Lot has convinced the two angelic strangers not to spend the night in the Sodom town square, a violent mob surrounds his house (Gen 19:2-8). In an attempt to appease the crowd, Lot comes up with a brilliant idea: "Here, take my two virgin daughters instead." Isn't Lot supposed to be the only righteous guy in Sodom? How does his righteousness fit with his willingness to have his daughters raped?[3] The text never condemns Lot for his brutal proposal, so it makes not only Lot but also his God seem misogynistic. Is the God of the Old Testament sexist?

As Israel was moving into the Promised Land, God commanded them to utterly wipe out the people of that land, the Canaanites (Josh 10:40). While the Canaanites were the bad guys (Deut 9:5), it still sounds like genocide. What kind of God would command such a slaughter? God seemed to value the Israelites more than the Canaanites. Is the God of the Old Testament racist?

Problematic texts such as these have contributed to a negative perception of God that is also found in popular culture.[4]

God the Cosmic Causer of Catastrophes

One of Gary Larson's most famous *The Far Side* cartoons depicts God sitting at his computer, which is displaying an image of an innocent-looking guy strolling along a sidewalk (with the standard Larsonian buckteeth).[5] A grand piano hangs precariously, just inches over the guy's head, supported only by a few thin ropes. God watches with his hand hovering over the keyboard, his index finger about to strike the "SMITE" key.

Larson's portrayal of God is funny, but also tragic. Tragic because it strikes a little too close to home for readers of the Old Testament as we encounter texts that describe how God smites, strikes, slays and even slaughters.

We don't need to look far to find other examples of negative portrayals of God in popular culture. In *Bruce Almighty*, Bruce (Jim Carrey), in a fit of suicidal depression because he lost the anchor job to Evan Baxter (Steve Carell), screams to God, "Smite me, O mighty smiter!" Interestingly, the prophet Elijah made a similar request to God ("It is enough; now, O LORD, take away my life"; 1 Kings 19:4).[6] Apparently, both Bruce and Elijah seemed to think that smiting is part of God's job description. While we could argue that Bruce didn't really know God very well, we can't apply that logic to Elijah. After all, God liked him (Elijah, not Bruce) enough to swoop him up directly into heaven

(2 Kings 2:11). So, is smiting really part of God's nature?

In an episode from the first season of *The Simpsons*, Bart's Sunday school teacher concludes the lesson with "and that's why God causes train wrecks."[7] While viewers aren't provided with the actual reasons, the teacher's perception of God as a cosmic causer of catastrophes seems to follow in the same vein as *The Far Side* and *Bruce Almighty*.

A "Megalomaniacal, Sadomasochistic, Capriciously Malevolent Bully"?

While we might be tempted not to take these negative popular portrayals seriously because of their comical nature, it is difficult to brush aside quickly the view of atheist Richard Dawkins. In his bestselling book *The God Delusion*, he writes,

> The God of the Old Testament is arguably the most unpleasant character in all fiction: jealous and proud of it; a petty, unjust, unforgiving control-freak; a vindictive, bloodthirsty ethnic cleanser; a misogynistic, homophobic, racist, infanticidal, genocidal, filicidal, pestilential, megalomaniacal, sadomasochistic, capriciously malevolent bully.[8]

While I don't agree with Dawkins's conclusions, his exaggerated tone does make for interesting reading, which explains its sales success. The fact that Dawkins's book has become an international bestseller indicates that he has touched a nerve.

The title of Christopher Hitchens's 2007 bestseller expresses a similar anti-God sentiment rather provocatively: *God Is Not Great: How Religion Poisons Everything.*[9] Perhaps no atheist writers since Bertrand Russell have made such a splash in popular culture as Dawkins and Hitchens. Larson, Bruce, *The Simpsons*, Dawkins and Hitchens all seem to view God negatively.

A negative perspective on God can even be found in the realm of insurance terminology. What is the legal term for disastrous events outside human control such as floods, earthquakes, tornadoes and hurricanes? "Acts of God." While this terminology doesn't necessarily preclude God doing good or kind acts, the lack of a negative qualifier (*"destructive* acts of God") suggests that when God acts, he wreaks havoc.

I realize that *The Far Side* and *The Simpsons* do not always depict God as a cosmic smiter and that Morgan Freeman's incarnation of God in the *Bruce/Evan Almighty* films is quite compelling.[10] But these negative portrayals of God are not unusual within contemporary culture. And while some of the comic divine portrayals are not as negative, writers such as Dawkins and Hitchens approach the subject in a highly polemical manner. Their brutal critiques of God demand a response.

Impeaching God

On August 8, 1974, I was playing outside with my brothers and friends on a hot summer night when we were called inside to watch something historic on TV. We wondered what could possibly be more important than smashing home runs into our neighbors' windows. (Someone clearly needed to sort out their priorities.) The parents informed us that the president was about to resign. We replied, "So what?" The voice of authority spoke: *"Come inside and watch TV!"* We watched as Richard Nixon told the nation that he would step down from the presidency. What was more shocking than the resignation itself, however, was the fact that the U.S. president was a criminal.

When the most powerful man in the world is not good, we ought to be concerned, but if the ruler of the cosmos is not good, that is even more deeply disturbing. We could say that Dawkins and Hitchens essentially "impeach" God by simply choosing not to believe in him. They remove God from power and attempt to convince others that God is bad and that worship of God is a delusion. We need to examine carefully not only these accusations of Dawkins and others but also the biblical texts they use to argue their points.

It would be deeply troubling if the ruler of the cosmos were in fact angry, sexist and racist. It would be particularly disturbing for the many individuals who have been victims of violence, sexism or racism. While the God of the Old Testament does get angry, what characterizes him is love. While he may seem sexist, he is highly affirming of women. While he may seem racist, he is hospitable toward all people. And, as the rest of this book will show, the Bible supports these conclusions.

God with Long, Wavy Gray Hair

What makes all these negative images of God particularly problematic for me is that they focus on my subject, the Old Testament. The God portrayed by Larson doesn't look like Jesus (no long, wavy brown hair), but rather resembles the Old Testament version (long, wavy *gray* hair). Jesus never smites anyone; in fact he seems to be averse to the whole smiting thing (Mt 5:39; Lk 22:49-51), but sometimes it seems that the Old Testament God can't keep his finger off the smite key (Ex 3:20; Num 25:17; Deut 7:2).[11] Jesus calms the storm (Mk 4:39), but the God of the Old Testament sends natural disasters (Ex 32:35; 2 Sam 24:15).[12]

Although Dawkins is repulsed by the Old Testament God, he likes Jesus: "Jesus is a huge improvement over the cruel ogre of the Old Testament."[13] He even wrote an article titled "Atheists for Jesus."[14] His attacks are clearly more focused on the God of Old Testament than the God of the New Testament. While I disagree with a lot of what Dawkins says, I will grant his point that the portrayal of God in the Old Testament can be disturbing. Even more to the point, Dawkins's list of divine characteristics includes many of the negative perceptions of God that trouble readers of the Old Testament. In a 2009 *Atlantic* article adapted from his book *The Evolution of God*, Robert Wright makes a similar point as he contrasts the "belligerent" and "often harsh" God of the Old Testament with the more loving version of the New Testament: "Jesus came along and set a different tone."[15]

There are numerous passages that people use to support their perspective that God is angry, sexist and racist. For those of us who read the Old Testament regularly, when we encounter these texts we are concerned, perplexed and, perhaps, tempted to ignore them. While I applaud Dawkins for bringing these problems into the open for discussion, I don't agree with his conclusions. He simply isn't reading his Bible well.

The Old Testament God vs. the New Testament God

After recalling the question that began this chapter, a careful reader could say to me, "You are doing the same thing as Dawkins—not reading your Bible well."

I confess that I am guilty.

A reading that sets up a contrast between a loving Old Testament God and a harsh New Testament God is a dramatic misreading of the Bible. However, a reading that does the opposite, contrasting the mean Old Testament God with the nice New Testament God, is also grossly inaccurate. But the initial question of this chapter and the following discussion were necessary to set up two general observations about biblical interpretation.

First, it is easy to misrepresent Scripture to make a point. We don't need to read Dawkins or other atheists to encounter people distorting the Bible to make a point because, unfortunately, many preachers and teachers of Scripture are also guilty of this. One of the easiest ways to misrepresent Scripture is just to ignore problematic texts. Because Bible teachers so frequently avoid certain texts when writers like Dawkins discuss them, it can seem that atheists are reading the Bible more carefully than people who view it as the Word of God.

Within this book, I will emphasize positive aspects of God's character because the Old Testament repeatedly describes God in this manner. But if I am to be faithful to the whole Old Testament, I will also need to examine other texts, even ones that appear to undermine my arguments. Dawkins does not do this. He simply avoids texts that speak of God favorably. To avoid misrepresenting the Bible, we need to look at many texts, to study passages on both sides of an issue and to read texts within their context. This type of reading will involve work, but the result will be well worth the effort as our understanding of God is profoundly deepened.

My second observation about biblical interpretation is that it is tempting to over-represent the differences between the two testaments, to the point of perceiving two separate gods. When I speak about "the God of the Old Testament," it may seem that I am implying there is a dichotomy. I don't actually believe that the Old Testament God is different from the New Testament God, but I am aware that both in popular culture and within the church, a difference is perceived.

The dichotomized portrayal of a mean Old Testament God and a nice New Testament God has a long history. In early Christianity, Marcion (c. A.D. 80–160) taught that there were two distinct gods. The God of the Old Testament was a harsh god of law and justice, while the God of the New Testament was a benevolent god of mercy and salvation. Marcion rejected the Old Testament as Christian Scripture, a conclusion that followed naturally from his view of the God it portrayed. We can see some of the attraction of Marcion's views (if we do not study the Old Testament), and Marcion's church became quite large in the second century.

Fortunately, for those of us who love the Old Testament, Marcion's views were deemed heretical by the church in the mid-second century. However, forms of the Marcionite heresy, with its anti-Old Testament perspective, still persist today, with the implication that many Christians do not read the Old Testament and appreciate what it has to offer. To overcome the legacy of Marcionism, we need to look more carefully at the Old Testament and read it alongside the New Testament, which is exactly what I hope to do in this book.

Names of God: Yahweh and Jesus

To understand the nature of the God of both testaments, a good place to start is to look at divine names in the Bible.[16] God is called many names and titles in the Old Testament. For something as simple as a name, the conversation quickly becomes complicated in the Hebrew (the language of the Old Testament) with plural forms for a single God, pronominal suffixes and combination forms, but here I will be brief and only mention a few of the more significant names.[17]

The Bible first calls God simply "God," *elohim* (Gen 1:1). He is referred to by this name frequently throughout the Old Testament (approximately 2,600 times).[18] God is also called either *adon* or *adonai*, "Lord" (Gen 15:2), over four hundred times in the Old Testament.

God's personal name, however, in the Old Testament is Yahweh (in Hebrew, יהוה). Traditionally, it has been spelled "Jehovah" in English, but more recently it might be spelled without vowels as YHWH. In modern English Bibles, this name is typically translated as "the Lord."[19] While the Bible includes a variety of divine names, God is called Yahweh far more than any other name in Scripture, over 6,800 times. When he introduced himself to Moses, God basically said, "Please, call me Yahweh" (Ex 3:15).[20] It is significant that God tells his people to call him by a name (Yahweh) and not a title (the Lord). So, when speaking about the God of the Old Testament, I will refer to him by his name, Yahweh.

Jesus is referred to in many ways in the New Testament, including "Son of Man" (Mt 8:20), "Son of David" (Mt 1:1), "Immanuel" (Mt 1:23) and "Lord" (Mt 7:21). More than five hundred times in the New Testament, Jesus is called "Christ," but his personal name, lest we forget, is simply "Jesus," and he was called this far more than either "Lord" or "Christ," almost a thousand times (958). So, when speaking about the God of the New Testament, I will use the name Jesus.

Just to be clear about theology, I believe not only that God the Father, Son and Holy Spirit are one, but also that Jesus and Yahweh are essentially one, but here it will be convenient to speak of God in the Old Testament as Yahweh and God in the New Testament as Jesus. I would hope this practice is not controversial, since I am simply following the conventions for divine names established in the two testaments. While the New Testament often refers to "God" generally and to the specific members of the divine Trinity (the Father, the Son, the Spirit), the divine name used most often in the New Testament is "Jesus," and this provides a good parallel to the Old Testament's usage of Yahweh.

Because I teach graduate students, many of whom are older than I am, I ask them to call me Dave. I am surprised how many of them persist in referring to me by titles (professor, doctor, doc, sir). I realize that students often use titles as a sign of respect, and non-Western traditions place a much higher value on that than mine does, but it is difficult not to feel that the practice of referring to me with a title keeps students at a distance. When a student who had called me Dr. Lamb finally calls me Dave, the relationship has shifted toward friendship.

I certainly think that it is appropriate in many settings to call God "God," "the Lord" or "Christ," but I am surprised at how infrequently Christians use "Yahweh" or even "Jesus," the two names the Bible uses most often for God. When we don't use personal names for God, an aspect of the relationship is lost.[21] The biblical pattern of referring to God primarily as Yahweh in the Old Testament and Jesus in the New Testament tells us that God wants to be on a first-name basis with his people. This model of intimacy in relationship between God and his people characterizes both testaments.

Jesus Loved the Old Testament

People who overdichotomize the two testaments seem to forget one important fact: the Bible of Jesus was the Old Testament. His value for the Old Testament can be seen in how frequently he referred to it. At the beginning of his ministry Jesus quoted Deuteronomy three times in the wilderness to Satan (Lk 4:4, 8, 12; Deut 6:13, 16; 8:3), and he quoted the Psalms as his final words on the cross (Mt 27:46; Ps 22:1). Throughout his entire ministry Jesus constantly mentioned the Old Testament law, the Prophets and the Psalms (for example, Lk 7:27; 10:26; 18:31; 19:46; 20:17; 22:37; 24:44). Jesus loved the Old Testament.

What is particularly relevant for this discussion, however, is that Jesus used the Old Testament to describe God. His description of God as a vineyard owner (Mt 21:33) came straight out of Isaiah 5:1-2. When Jesus told a scribe that the Lord our God is one (Mk 12:29), he quoted Deuteronomy 6:4. When the high priest asked him if he is the Christ, Jesus first stated, "I am," an allusion to God's Old Testament name, Yahweh (Ex 3:14), and then he combined two Old Testament texts into a prophecy that they will see him as the Son of Man seated at God's right hand (Ps 110:1), coming in the clouds of heaven (Dan 7:13). Jesus frequently used Old Testament images to describe both himself and God as a bridegroom (Is 62:5; Mk 2:19), as a shepherd (Ezek 34; Jn 10:11) and as a king (Ps 47; Mt 18:23). Jesus not only knew the Old Testament, he also identified completely with its God.

Jesus also understood that the main thing that God expects of humans is love. To support the idea that God is primarily concerned about love, where did Jesus go? The Old Testament. In his response to a question about which command was the greatest, Jesus mentioned two from the Old Testament (Deut 6:5; Lev 19:18); the first one tells us to love God completely and the second tells us to love our neighbor as ourselves (Mk 12:30-31).[22] While Christians unfortunately have a tendency to focus on other issues, Jesus knew that Yahweh is a God of love.

How Do Negative Perceptions of Yahweh Affect Readers of the Old Testament?

It is easy to forget that the God of both testaments is primarily concerned about love, and negative images of Yahweh can contribute to this memory loss. Negative perceptions of God, stemming from erroneous interpretations of the Old Testament, not only affect non-Christians who refuse to believe in him because of their misperceptions, they also affect Christians, in both obvious and subtle ways. So let's look at a few of the spiritual problems that emerge from distorted perceptions of Yahweh.

Our image of God will directly affect how we either pursue or avoid God. If we believe that the God of the Old Testament is really harsh, unfair and cruel, we won't want anything to do with him. Who would want to have a close relationship with a divine version of Adolf Hitler? Dawkins and Hitchens not only want to avoid God, but also have become "evangelists" spreading the good news that theism is delusional.

Interestingly, the people in the Old Testament who knew God best desperately desired to be with him: Enoch and Noah (Gen 5:24; 6:9), Abraham and Jacob (Gen 18:1-5; 32:26), Moses and Joshua (Ex 33:11, 15-16), Deborah and Hannah (Judg 4:4; 5:1-31; 1 Sam 1:10-12; 2:1-10), David and Solomon (1 Sam 13:14; 1 Kings 8:23-61), Elijah and Elisha (1 Kings 19:10; 2 Kings 6:16-20). These individuals must have understood something about God that we don't. It is my hope that, as we examine both their God and their lives, we will become more like them and our desire to draw near to God will increase.

A negative perception about God could also affect a person's passion for reading Scripture. Many Christians feel guilty for not reading their Bibles, so it doesn't help that when they finally get around to doing it, they encounter a command not to wear wool and linen together followed by a command to wear tassels on the corners of their clothes (Deut 22:11-12). Hmm. Why does God care about our attire, particularly something as mundane as interwoven garments? (Especially when we know that the devil wears Prada.) Even a pious believer might decide no longer to bother to read the Old Testament after discovering commands like these. (We'll discuss this command about clothes in chapter six.)

Interestingly, the author of Psalm 119 does not view God's commands as obscure, bizarre or irrelevant. In fact, the psalmist uses language that is almost embarrassingly effusive toward the law: "My soul is consumed with longing for your ordinances at all times" (Ps 119:20). This psalm sounds more like romantic poetry than a worship hymnal. And there's a lot more where that came from: "Oh, how I love your law! It is my meditation all day long" (Ps 119:97). It is fascinating that the longest chapter in the entire Bible is devoted to singing the praises of God's law. The psalmist was obsessed with Scripture. The psalmist knew God and God's Word well, and that fueled a passion for reading it. Greater familiarity with Yahweh and the Old Testament should not discourage us from reading the Bible, but increase our love for it.

Our image of God will also affect what we think God's followers should be like. If God really were angry, sexist and racist, it would follow that Christians would be as well. The issues of violence, race and gender are some of the most pressing and controversial ones facing the world today. A lot has been written about how popular perceptions of Christians and the church affect popular perceptions of God. Unfortunately, the church is generally perceived in popular culture as contributing to the problem and not as part of the solution.

Compared to other ancient Near Eastern literature, the Old Testament is shockingly progressive in its portrayals of divine love, acceptance of foreigners and affirmation of women. The Old Testament was not only divinely inspired, it was also culturally engaged. As we become aware of the context of the Old Testament, the problematic portrayals of Yahweh don't magically disappear, but they do become more understandable. And as we study the cultural contexts alongside the numerous passages that portray Yahweh more favorably, not only does a highly attractive God emerge, but God's followers also appear as people we would want to emulate, not as hotheads, chauvinists and bigots.

God Behaving Badly?

The rest of this book will discuss many problematic passages in the Old Testament in which God appears to behave badly. It will examine negative perceptions of the God of the Old Testament, with each chapter focusing on a different issue. I realize that some divine perceptions are more controversial (angry, sexist, racist and violent) than others (legalistic, rigid and distant), but all find some basis in the Old Testament and most appear in some form in Dawkins's quote.

Since we can find a verse to say almost anything, I will look at many biblical texts across the diverse genres of Old Testament literature in an attempt to find patterns of descriptions of divine behavior and to characterize the God of the Old Testament as generally as possible. I will not only discuss how pervasive these perceptions are in popular culture, but also interact with relevant ancient Near Eastern texts to understand the issue within its own historical context. I will end each chapter looking at a relevant incident from the Gospels, showing how the particular characteristic of Yahweh is also manifested in the behavior of Jesus. It is my hope that your love not only for the Old Testament but also for the God of both testaments will deepen as you read these chapters.

2

ANGRY OR LOVING?

Whenever you read from the Old Testament, God is always crabby and snarky to everyone, but the New Testament isn't about anger at all—it's about love."

This observation is made by Sam to her mother (Boopsie) in a 2009 *Doonesbury* comic strip (May 31) after she heard Rev. Sloan reading from the Bible about the wrath of God. Sam's statement captures the essence of the supposed conflict between the anger of Yahweh in the Old Testament and the love of Jesus in the New Testament. As we look at Old Testament passages focused on anger and love, we will have to decide whether Sam listens badly, Rev. Sloan reads badly or Yahweh behaves badly. So, is the God of the Old Testament really angry, crabby and snarky?

A Lightning Bolt from God
Two men are playing golf, a pastor and an elder from his church. The pastor tees off first and strikes a beautiful drive straight down the fairway. The elder hooks the ball badly into the lake and yells, "#@*&%! I missed!" The pastor says to the elder,

"Careful, or God will strike you with lightning."

On the next hole, a par-three, the pastor's 7-iron lands five feet from the cup. The elder's tee shot flies over the green into the bunker, and he shouts, "#@*&%! I missed!" The pastor warns him, "Careful, or God will strike you with lightning."

On the next hole, the pastor smashes his drive three hundred yards, and it rolls to within ten feet for a potential eagle putt. The elder slices his tee shot far into the woods and again exclaims, "#@*&%! I missed!" Immediately the clouds darken, the wind picks up, and a lightning bolt flashes down and hits not the foul-mouthed elder, but the pastor.

The elder looks up and hears a voice from heaven exclaiming, "#@*&%! I missed!"[1]

If there is one popular image that instantly flashes to mind on the topic of God and anger it would have to be being struck by lightning for doing something (usually trivial) that makes God mad.[2] A quick Google search of "lightning" and "God" revealed many versions of this joke (variations involve baseball and hunting).

In chapter one, I stated that Yahweh is primarily concerned with love, but the Old Testament also speaks frequently about Yahweh becoming angry and sometimes even killing people in his anger. Doesn't that undermine the idea of Yahweh as loving? This chapter will discuss the tension between divine love and divine anger. We might not completely resolve the problem, but by looking at relevant Old Testament passages we will better understand why Yahweh becomes angry (he doesn't become angry over swearing) and how his anger makes sense.

Support for the view that Yahweh is a God of anger can be found in the story of Uzzah and the Ark, so that's a good place to start.

Why Did Yahweh Smite Uzzah?

The Ark of the Covenant had fallen into the hands of the Philistines (1 Sam 4–5), and David was finally bringing back the lost ark to Jerusalem:

> David again gathered **all** the chosen men of Israel, thirty thousand. And David arose and went with **all** the people who were with him from Baale-judah to bring up from there the ark of God, which is called by the name of the Lord of hosts who sits enthroned on the cherubim. And they carried the ark of God on a new cart and brought it out of the house of Abinadab, which was on the hill. And Uzzah and Ahio, the sons of Abinadab, were driving the new cart, with the ark of God, and Ahio went before the ark.
>
> And David and **all** the house of Israel were making merry before the Lord, with songs and lyres and harps and tambourines and castanets and cymbals. And when they came to the threshing floor of Nacon, Uzzah put out his hand to the ark of God and took hold of it, for the oxen stumbled. And the *anger* of the Lord was kindled against Uzzah, and God struck him down there because of his error, and he died there beside the ark of God. And David was *angry* because the Lord had burst forth against Uzzah. And that place is called Perez-uzzah, to this day. (2 Sam 6:1-8)

(When I quote from biblical passages, I will often highlight important repeated words with **bold** or *italics* in the text to make them stand out clearly, such as "**all**," or "Lord" or "*angry*" from this passage.)

The festivities basically included a big parade with dancing, celebrating and a marching band. Suddenly, the cart carrying the ark shook as the oxen that were pulling it stumbled. Uzzah, one of the men walking alongside it, reached out to stabilize the ark, but Yahweh got angry at Uzzah and instantly killed him.

What prompted this divine display of rage? Wasn't Uzzah doing a good thing by protecting the ark from tipping over? Surely whatever he was doing didn't deserve a death sentence. Why did God have to kill him? Even David, a man after God's own heart, got mad at Yahweh for the outburst. Stories like this give the God of the Old Testament a bad reputation.

While the story of Uzzah and the ark is deeply troubling, as we begin to examine the causes of God's anger it becomes more understandable. Yahweh was angry here for three main reasons.

Carrying the ark. First, Yahweh told the Israelites how to carry the ark, and they weren't obeying. Yahweh told them that they were not to transport the ark on a cart, but it was to be carried by the priests on poles through rings on the side of the ark (Ex 25:10-15; Num 4:15; 7:7-9; Deut 10:8). Yahweh's directions were not found just in one obscure text, but he made it very clear throughout the law how the ark was to be transported. Previously in the narrative, the ark had always been carried the right way by Israel (Deut 31:9, 25; Josh 3:3, 15, 17; 4:9, 10, 18; 6:6; 8:33; 1 Sam 4:4).

Yahweh's concern with proper protocols for ark transportation may seem a bit OCD (like symptoms of obsessive-compulsive disorder) to our postmodern, highly casual sensibilities, but an analogy might help us understand the need for precaution. Handling the ark was inherently dangerous, like handling radioactive materials. If people do not use proper precaution when transporting plutonium, people die. The U.S. Nuclear Regulatory Commission (NRC) gives even more-detailed guidelines about transporting radioactive materials than the Pentateuch does about transporting the ark. (Check out the NRC's website the next time you need to transport plutonium.[3]) Personally, I'm glad the NRC is a bit OCD when it comes to moving nuclear waste through my neighborhood. (BP wasn't OCD enough when drilling for oil in the Gulf of Mexico on the Deepwater Horizon rig in April 2010, and people died.) God gave the Israelites guidelines to protect them from being reckless with the ark, because God is more powerful than plutonium.

While God had told them in Exodus, Numbers and Deuteronomy, maybe they forgot, or perhaps they hadn't been meditating on these books recently, so they didn't know how Yahweh wanted the ark transported. Well, actually it would have been difficult to forget how the ark was meant to be carried, because it had two rings on each side for the poles, so that every time they looked at it they would be reminded that Yahweh wanted it to be borne on the shoulders of the priests. We know that they knew the correct way to carry it, because three months after the tragedy with Uzzah, they carried the ark all the way to Jerusalem just as God had told them to transport it (2 Sam 6:13). The Chronicles version of the incident makes it clear that Yahweh was angry because they weren't carrying it properly (1 Chron 15:11-13).

The timing of Yahweh's anger is also significant here. The text repeatedly informs us that "all" Israel was present (2 Sam 6:1, 2, 5); a crowd of 30,000 people was watching this parade. With an audience of the entire nation, Yahweh did not want to send the message that obedience was optional, since it was disobedience that led to the loss of the ark earlier and the slaughter by Philistines of 30,000 Israelites (1 Sam 4:10). Anger displayed in situations of disobedience gets people's attention. Yahweh's extreme display of anger certainly got the attention of David and the rest of the nation. After the incident with Uzzah, the ark was always carried the right way (2 Sam 6:13; 15:29; 1 Kings 2:26; 8:3).

So it makes sense that Yahweh was mad because the Israelites should have known better. While Uzzah's death seems
harsh, Yahweh had warned them. He told them if anyone
touched the ark, he or she would die (Num 4:15). Uzzah should
not have touched it.

Throughout the Old Testament it was always serious and
even dangerous for individuals to come close to the presence of
Yahweh (Ex 3:5; 19:16; 33:20; Judg 6:22-23; 1 Kings 19:11-12;
Job 41:10; Ps 76:7; Mal 3:2). If Israel's disobedience were the
only reason for Yahweh's anger, we might think that he was
being petty and harsh, but the next two reasons for Yahweh's
anger help explain the severity of the crime.

Riding in the trunk. The second reason Yahweh became mad
is that their decision to transport the ark on a cart was not only
disobedient, it was also insulting. To understand how a method
of transportation could be insulting, we need to recall what the
ark represented: the presence of God (Ex 25:22; Lev 16:2; 1 Sam
4:4). Therefore, it warranted extraordinary care. What the law
prescribed for the conveyance of the ark was basically a litter (a
chair or throne for a distinguished person supported by people
carrying poles on each side). Royalty was frequently honored
by this method of transport, going back to ancient China and
Egypt. King Solomon was carried around on a litter (Song 3:7)
as was the Syrian ruler Antiochus V (2 Macc 9:8). It was important for Yahweh's symbolic presence to be treated in a royal
fashion because he was their God and King. David needed not
to forget that even though he was king over Israel, Yahweh was
sovereign over him and the nation.

Litters were for rulers, but carts or wagons were for things
(offerings: Num 7:3; tabernacle equipment: Num 7:7-8; grain:
Amos 2:13). *Never* for royalty.[4] Placing the ark on a cart was an
insult. They were celebrating its return, but by putting the ark

on a cart, they were in essence saying the ark was cargo. Also, it was the Philistines who came up with the idea of the ark-cart (1 Sam 6:8-11), so instead of following God's law, they were following the example of their enemies. It shouldn't surprise us that God was mad.

When I was in college, if my friends and I were going to the movies and we didn't have enough spaces in cars, sometimes I would ride in the trunk. I usually found it relatively comfortable (trunks were bigger then). I liked to crack open the trunk and hang a limp hand out the back to get a reaction from tailgaters. (I no longer recommend this behavior.) Why don't we put people in the trunk? Trunks and carts are for cargo (or dead bodies). Front seats are for humans. Litters are for kings and the ark of Yahweh.

What would it be like if the U.S. president were to come to a town for a parade and the city council asked him to ride in the trunk of a car? He or she would be offended and almost certainly angry. That's basically what Israel was doing with the ark. They should have known better. It was an insult to Yahweh, so he became mad. They needed to treat the ark not simply as a box, because it had a profound symbolic meaning as the presence of God in their midst. It deserved respect. But the ark represented even more than that.

Losing the ark. Third, Israel's lack of respect toward the ark was symptomatic of a lack of concern for their relationship with God, and that made him mad too. The ark symbolized not only the presence of Yahweh, but also the covenantal relationship between God and his people. The text frequently calls it the Ark of the Covenant of Yahweh (Num 10:33; 14:44; Deut 10:8; 31:9; Josh 3:3, 11; 1 Sam 4:3, 4, 5; 1 Kings 3:15; 6:19; Jer 3:16). The ark contained a copy of the Ten Commandments (Deut 10:1-5), which told Israel what their covenant with Yahweh involved: to love God and to love their neighbor.

In general, the Old Testament tells the story of a one-sided relationship, in which one partner (Yahweh) is more committed than the other (Israel) to the covenant. Often God is patient and doesn't punish instantly, but eventually he may need to take drastic measures to get their attention. Because of their perpetual disrespect for the ark of Yahweh and the public nature of this transportation ceremony, it was now a critical time and it warranted sudden punishment. Yahweh valued the covenant with his people so highly that he wanted to communicate the message that he would not tolerate disrespect for the object that symbolized that relationship.

Those of us who are married have a similar covenantal symbolic object: a wedding ring. I once lost mine for almost two months. I hated being without it because its absence suggested not only that I was irresponsible, but also that I didn't value my relationship with Shannon. Eventually, our dog, Tiglath (named after the Assyrian ruler, 2 Kings 15:29), lost his tennis ball underneath the washbasin in our laundry room. He was too scared of the washbasin to go retrieve it (he's only part retriever), so Shannon got down on the floor, fought past the sea of endless tennis shoes, reached through the concoction of soccer mud, grass clippings, canine fur and laundry lint, stretched out for the ball and found what? My missing ring. It had slipped off my finger while I was giving Tig a bath. Later that day, we had a Dave's-ring-is-back celebration, although ours wasn't as elaborate as King David's the-ark-is-back celebration (and I kept my clothes on; see 2 Sam 6:14, 20).

For a long time after finding the ring, I was extra careful with it because I didn't want to lose it again. Although Yahweh wasn't the one who had just lost the ark, apparently he felt similarly about it. Yahweh's people had just lost their "ring" (the ark) to the Philistines because of their evil deeds and their careless attitude toward the ark. Yahweh didn't want them to lose it again and, like my concern for my ring, he wanted them to be more careful with it. His display of anger toward Uzzah was effective. For the remainder of the monarchy, they not only carried the ark the right way, but there was never a "sequel" of the incident of the lost ark.[5]

From the Uzzah incident, we learn that Yahweh gets mad to protect his law, his honor and his relationship with his people. Would you want to follow a God that wasn't passionate about his relationship with you? Each of these reasons seems valid. Now we can look at other examples of divine anger in the Old Testament.

Slow to Anger

Anger plays an important role in the story of the Exodus. The Hebrew word *'ap* translated as "anger" literally means "nose" (perhaps because anger was thought to be focused in the face, with the nose becoming red). The word appears ten times in the book of Exodus, always in reference to Yahweh or Moses (Ex 4:14; 11:8; 15:8; 22:24; 32:10, 11, 12, 19, 22; 34:6). Let's look at what makes God and Moses mad in Exodus.

At the beginning of the book, Israel has already been enslaved for hundreds of years in Egypt, and Pharaoh begins to undertake a draconian birth-control measure for the Hebrews: male infanticide (Ex 1:8-22). In the midst of this brutal oppression, the Israelites cry out to Yahweh (Ex 2:23). The text tells us that God hears their groans and remembers his covenant with Abraham (Ex 2:24-25). Yahweh then begins the process of rescuing his people from their bondage by choosing a leader for the task, Moses.

During the interaction at the burning bush, Moses offers a series of five objections to Yahweh:

1. Who am I?

2. Who are you?

3. The Israelites won't listen to me!

4. I can't speak well!

5. Please pick someone else! (Ex 3:11, 13; 4:1, 10, 13)

(Exactly what I would have said if someone asked me to be in charge of rescuing a few million slaves from the greatest empire on earth.)

So, how does Yahweh respond to Moses' reluctance? He listens to the first four objections and responds graciously, but eventually he gets angry (Ex 4:14). We need to note three things here about Yahweh's anger.

First, Yahweh didn't smite anyone in his anger. Sometimes Yahweh smites, but often he doesn't (for example, Job 42:7; Ps 78:21; Is 12:1; 54:8). Yahweh expressed his anger and Moses was certainly aware of it, and his anger achieved the desired result. After Yahweh's outburst, Moses offered no more objections, and he dutifully headed back to Egypt to start the process of deliverance (Ex 4:18-20), which leads to the next point.

Second, Yahweh became angry because he wanted to deliver his people, but Moses didn't want to help. The Israelite nation was struggling under oppressive enslavement, but Moses didn't want to get involved. God was not only mad that his people were slaves, but also that Moses didn't seem to care that his own extended family was suffering. Later, on Mount Sinai, Yahweh told Moses that his people were not to oppress or take advantage of widows, orphans or aliens, because they were aliens in Egypt, and if they did, Yahweh's wrath would burn hot against them (Ex 22:21-24).

In the book of Amos, Yahweh got angry at Judah for similar reasons, so angry that he roared like a lion (Amos 1:2; 3:4, 8). In Amos, Yahweh's wrath targeted the things that someone with a concern for justice would ideally want targeted: oppression (Amos 1:6, 9; 2:12; 3:9; 4:1; 8:4, 6), violence (Amos 1:3, 11, 13; 2:7; 8:4) and injustice (Amos 2:6-7; 5:15; 6:12). Compared to the things that cause me to get mad (someone taking too long in the bathroom or eating the last of the mint-chip ice cream), Yahweh's reasons for wrath seem more legitimate: the elimination of oppression, violence and injustice. Ultimately, in these contexts God's wrath came from his compassion. This is a good thing. I should get angry about injustice like Yahweh.

Third, it took Yahweh a long time to get angry. He didn't get mad after the first, second, third or even fourth objection from Moses, but only after the fifth did he finally mad. Yahweh was slow to anger.

The "Long Nose" of the LORD

The idea that Yahweh gets angry slowly is emphasized throughout the Old Testament. Yahweh is repeatedly described as "slow to anger" (literally, "long-nosed"—one of the few similarities between God and myself). This description of Yahweh is not limited to a specific Old Testament book or Old Testament section but is found across the diverse genres of the Old Testament. It appears in historical contexts (Ex 34:6; Num 14:18; Neh 9:17), prophetic contexts (Joel 2:13; Jon 4:2; Nah 1:3) and poetic contexts (Ps 86:15; 103:8; 145:8).

Slowness to anger is so much a part of Yahweh's character, he includes it in his name. When Yahweh reveals himself to Moses on Mount Sinai, the text says Yahweh proclaimed his name to Moses, "Yahweh, Yahweh, a God merciful and gracious, slow to anger and abounding in steadfast love and faithfulness" (Ex 34:5-6).[6] In the Bible, names mean something significant, representing one's essence and character. Yahweh is God's first name in the Old Testament, but his full name speaks of his graciousness, patience and slowness to anger.

Ironically, Yahweh had just become furious at his people (Ex 32:10), which doesn't seem very patient of him . . . until you read the rest of the story. Yahweh's slowness to anger can be understood only in the context of the deliverance of his people from hundreds of years of oppression.

If I had just been freed from a lifetime of enslavement, I would hope it would put me in a permanent grateful mood, like a year-round Thanksgiving. But as soon as the Israelites get out of Egypt, they start complaining. When they see the approaching chariots, they complain that Yahweh brought them out to kill them (Ex 14:11). They complain about bitter water, about a lack of food and about a lack of water (Ex 15:24; 16:3; 17:2). The needs that the Israelites have for protection, food and water are certainly legitimate, yet in each complaint they assume the worst about their God—that Yahweh is secretly plotting their deaths. Their grumbling betrays a lack of trust, despite all that Yahweh has done so far to rescue them. But Yahweh shows great patience toward his people. Before Mount Sinai, the only people in the book that he gets mad at are the Egyptians (Ex 15:7-8).

God does get mad at Israel eventually, but this reaction is reasonable given the context. The fifth complaint of the Israelites is addressed to Aaron about Moses' lengthy absence with a request for Aaron to "make gods for us," so he makes them a golden calf (Ex 32:1-4). Aaron apparently sees nothing wrong with this behavior, despite the fact that he and all the people just promised to follow all Yahweh's commands (Ex 24:3, 7), which include specific prohibitions against the creation of and worship of idols and other gods (Ex 20:3-5).

The Sinai covenant was like the wedding between Yahweh and Israel, in which they committed to be faithful to each other (Ex 19:5-6; 24:3-8). But on the honeymoon the Israelites had sex with someone else. That seems like a legitimate cause for anger. So Yahweh's anger burns hot against his people, and he tells Moses that they will be destroyed (Ex 32:10). Fortunately for Israel, Moses convinces Yahweh to change his mind (Ex 32:11-14; see also chapter seven, "Rigid or Flexible?").

The Exodus pattern seems to generally fit the entire Old Testament: Yahweh delivers them. They complain. He is patient. They promise to obey. The first opportunity they get, they disobey. Yahweh eventually becomes angry and punishes them. The name "slow to anger" for Yahweh seems appropriate.

Recently, as we were about to fall asleep, we opened our windows to get some fresh spring air inside, but we were surprised to discover that the Daytona 500 was being held in our front lawn. Actually, it was just a Harley-Davidson accelerating on the road in front of our house,[7] but it woke up both my sons. I was furious. (I get mad just writing about it.)

It is easy to get mad instantly. We quickly become enraged if someone pulls in front of us on the road, throws trash on our lawn or makes us wait too long at a restaurant. For many of us, anger is a daily occurrence. Wrath comes quickly and easily. What is difficult is to get angry slowly. It takes patience. Yahweh is patient, but that's not all.

The Abundant, Enduring Steadfast Love of Yahweh

As noted above, the description of Yahweh as "slow to anger" first appears in the context of a divine name revealed after the golden calf incident (Ex 34:6). In the rest of the verse, Yahweh is also said to be "merciful," "gracious" and "abounding in steadfast love and faithfulness."

While all these descriptors sound positive, one in particular stands out: "steadfast love," or *hesed* in the Hebrew. Other translations render *hesed* as "lovingkindness," "kindness," "love" or "mercy." It is difficult to fully comprehend all the possible connotations of a word in another language, but *hesed* is the best kind of love one could imagine. It is the love of a devoted parent to a child from infancy to adulthood and beyond. It is the love of a committed spouse to her or his partner over decades of marriage. It is not a word used lightly for a relationship. In light of this, we can now make three observations about the *hesed* of Yahweh.

First, *hesed* in the Old Testament usually describes the behavior of Yahweh. The word occurs frequently in the Old Testament (251 times), and the vast majority of these are descriptions of Yahweh (179 times). Many of the occurrences appear in the Psalms (123), but Yahweh is characterized by *hesed* generally throughout the Old Testament and specifically in most Old Testament books. While Abraham had to wait for a son, while Jacob was fleeing his fratricidal brother and while Joseph was languishing in prison, they were all shown *hesed* by Yahweh (Gen 24:27; 32:10; 39:21). God gave Abraham a son in Isaac, he protected and blessed Jacob, and he made Joseph prosper, eventually promoting him over all Egypt. Yahweh is a god of steadfast love.

Second, not only is Yahweh loving, but his *hesed* is abundant. In the other eight Old Testament verses that describe Yahweh as "slow to anger," the immediate context includes formulaic language echoing Exodus 34:6-7, with the repetitions of the following words or phrases: "abounding in steadfast love (*hesed*)" (7 times), "merciful" (6), "gracious" (6), "faithful" (1), "forgiving" (2), "relenting from disaster" (2). Interestingly, the description for Yahweh that is most commonly linked with "slow to anger" is abundant *hesed* (Num 14:18; Neh 9:17; Ps 86:15; 103:8; 145:8; Joel 2:13; Jon 4:2). Yahweh's own name declares that he can be characterized by overwhelming *hesed*. Yahweh's abounding *hesed* combines with a variety of other positive attributes—mercy, grace, faithfulness and forgiveness—making him a deity worthy of worship.

Third, not only is Yahweh's *hesed* abundant, it is also enduring. The phrase "his steadfast love endures forever" occurs 42 times in the Old Testament to describe Yahweh. While 26 of these occur in one psalm (Ps 136, the *hesed* psalm), the other 16 are scattered around the Old Testament (1 Chron 16:34, 41; 2 Chron 5:13; 7:3, 6; 20:21; Ps 100:5; 106:1; 107:1; 118:1, 2, 3, 4, 29; Ezra 3:11; Jer 33:11). When Yahweh declared his name to Moses, he stated that while he punishes for three or four generations, his *hesed* continues for thousands of generations (Ex 34:7).[8] A similar idea of thousands of generations of steadfast love for obedience is expressed in the Ten Commandments (Ex 20:6) as well as in three other texts (Deut 7:9; 1 Chron 16:15; Ps 105:8). A thousand generations would last a long time (about 30,000 years). So, if you are a descendent of King David (he had quite a few, the main reason for all the "no vacancy" signs in Bethlehem during Jesus' birth), you are still reaping benefits from his steadfast obedience three millennia ago.

So Yahweh gets angry slowly and loves abundantly and enduringly, but you might be wondering about the Canaanites or the Egyptians. Did Yahweh abundantly love them?

Did Yahweh Abundantly Love the Canaanites and the Egyptians?

The issue of God's relationship with the Canaanites and the

Egyptians is problematic, and one we'll revisit in chapters four
and five, but a few points need to be made here in the context
of divine anger. While establishing the covenant with Abraham
(Gen 15:12-21), Yahweh informs him that his descendants will
be slaves for four hundred years.[9] (At that point I might have
asked Yahweh, "So how is this covenant a *good* thing?") In this
context Yahweh also mentions the Egyptians and the Canaanites. He tells Abraham that judgments will come upon both the
nation that oppresses Abraham's descendants (Egypt) and the
idolatrous people who live in Canaan (the Amorites, Canaanites, Perizzites and so on).

  While I understand why people advocate on behalf of the
Egyptians in Exodus (Why did God harden Pharaoh's heart?
Why did God drown them in the Red Sea?), when asking these
questions we need to remember the big picture. Egypt was the
most powerful nation on the planet and at the top of the Egyptian power "pyramid" stood Pharaoh. He was worshiped as a
god. The Egyptians were the ones enslaving and oppressing.
Feeling sorry for Egypt is like feeling sorry for Moe, from *Calvin and Hobbes*, the six-year-old bully who tortures Calvin during gym, steals his lunch money and calls him "Twinky." (Not
surprisingly, Moe also shaves.) Modern-day equivalents to
Moses' Pharaoh would be despots like Robert Mugabe or Kim
Jong-il, oppressive leaders that most of us would find it difficult
to feel compassion toward.

  We don't feel sorry for the bully but for the victim, which
relates to my big question about Egypt and Israel. Why did God
allow his own people to suffer so long under Egyptian oppression? Because he is a God that is slow to anger. He waited four
hundred years. My belly doesn't like to wait two minutes for the
chili to heat up in the microwave. It's hard to imagine waiting
for four hundred years for anything. One of the main purposes

of delaying divine judgment is that it gives people opportunities to repent. Because Yahweh delayed the judgment on Nineveh, they eventually repented, and he turned away from his anger (Jon 3:5-10).

Yahweh also waited to punish the Canaanites because, even though they were guilty already, their sin was not yet finished (Gen 15:16). So God waited four hundred years to punish the Egyptians and the Canaanites, and during this period his own people paid the price. Because Yahweh is slow to anger, his people were not only homeless but also slaves and victims of oppression. Eventually, Yahweh got angry at the crimes of Egypt and Canaan, and he finally delivered Israel from enslavement and provided them with a homeland. However, for four hundred years in Egypt, they paid the price for Yahweh's slowness to anger.

If We Avoid Them, They Won't Go Away

I won't be able to discuss in one chapter all the places in the Old Testament where Yahweh gets angry, but I've tried to focus on a few of the more problematic passages. I encourage you to look at some others on your own. Yahweh got angry at Balaam (Num 22:22), at Moses (Deut 3:26), at Solomon (1 Kings 11:9), at Job's friends (Job 42:7), at Israel (Judg 2:20; 2 Kings 17:18; Ps 106:40; Zech 7:12) and even at all the nations of the earth (Is 34:2).

Studying the divine anger sections of the Old Testament may not make us feel warm and fuzzy inside like meditating on Psalm 23, but it's important not to avoid these texts. It can be embarrassing for those of us who teach the Bible when other people talk about a story of God getting mad and we didn't even know it was in there. But beyond personal embarrassment, it will take some work to interpret these divine-anger texts correctly. Fear of tough texts won't help. If we avoid them, they won't go away. The only way to understand them is to read, study, discuss and teach them.

If you are troubled by passages in the Old Testament in which Yahweh got angry, here are three pieces of advice. First, ask why Yahweh got angry. Be open to finding a legitimate reason for his anger. In Uzzah's case, Yahweh was mad because his people weren't following his instructions and, as a result, weren't honoring the relationship. There will be a reason for Yahweh's anger. See if you can find it.

Second, read the whole context. Yahweh did get mad at Israel in Exodus 32, but only after he had freed them from slavery, rescued them from the Egyptian army, fed them with manna, provided water for them and met with them at Sinai. He was mad because they committed adultery on the honeymoon. Given the context, it makes sense that Yahweh got mad.

Third, have reasonable expectations. You won't be able to resolve all the problems. But some work will help you understand these passages better and save you embarrassment over your lack of biblical knowledge and over the behavior of God.

WWJW? (Who Would Jesus Whip?)

The *Doonesbury* strip quoted at the beginning of this chapter continues as Sam contrasts Jesus to the Old Testament God: "God's only son is this total pacifist—he wouldn't harm a flea. He's just this humble dude who's mellow to everyone—even the Romans. He only really snaps once, right?" Boopsie asks, "Who with, honey?" Sam answers, "The moneylenders, Mom!" Boopsie replies, "Oh, right. What is it about moneylenders?" Rev. Sloan finally chimes in, "They do seem to set people off, don't they?"

Sam brings up the most famous example of Jesus becoming angry, often called the "cleansing of the temple." The Gospel writers apparently thought it was important for the anger of Jesus to be emphasized, since all four of them include this incident (Mt 21:12-13; Mk 11:15-17; Lk 19:45-46; Jn 2:14-16). When Jesus saw what was going on in the temple, he made a whip to drive out not just the animals (cattle, sheep, doves) but also their humans (livestock traders and money changers).[10] (I had a whip when I was a kid, but Mom never let me use it on my brothers. I should have responded, "But Jesus used his whip on the money changers.") Jesus also dumped over their tables and coins.

Jesus was angry that people, particularly the Gentiles, were being deprived of the opportunity to pray and worship God. The livestock sellers and money changers were doing business in the court of the Gentiles, and Jesus specifically quoted Isaiah 56:7 that the temple was meant to be a house of prayer for all nations. Can you imagine trying to pray in the middle of the New York Stock Exchange? Jesus became furious because people were prevented from communing with their God. That seems like a good reason to get mad.

Interestingly, the night before he cleansed the temple, after his triumphal entry into Jerusalem, Jesus went into the temple and looked around at everything (Mk 11:11). He saw the tables of the money changers and smelled the "deposits" of the livestock, but he decided to wait until the next day to take action and display his wrath. Jesus, like Yahweh, was slow to anger.

While Jesus was clearly mad during the temple "cleansing," the only time the Gospels state explicitly that he was angry was when he healed the man with a withered hand (Mk 3:1-6). Jesus was angry at the Pharisees because they didn't want him to heal the man on the sabbath. Ironically, the Pharisees didn't want a healing on the sabbath, but they had no problem conspiring to kill Jesus on the sabbath. Amazingly, Jesus wasn't mad that the

Pharisees were plotting Christocide, but rather that they had hard hearts and didn't want him to show compassion on the man. Jesus' anger was totally legitimate. He and Yahweh both became angry at a lack of compassion.

Taking God's Mercy for Granted

So Jesus and Yahweh get angry, but Yahweh's angry responses still seem too extreme. I just wish God didn't kill people in his anger to punish them. At this point it will be helpful to reflect briefly on what the Bible says about sin and death. Even though it's not popular to talk about, both testaments teach that death is the just punishment for sin (Gen 2:17; Rom 6:23; Jas 1:15). So the death of Uzzah in the Old Testament and Ananias and Sapphira in the New Testament (Acts 5:1-11) really shouldn't shock us. We are surprised by these intense stories because the vast majority of the time that people sin, no one dies instantly, so when someone does, it seems unfair. If the wages of sin are death, why don't more people die immediately?

More people don't die instantly because God is gracious and slow to anger. He decides to delay the punishment for sin and give people opportunities to repent. While severe punishments should remind us that death is the natural consequence of sin, instead we think God is mean. While delayed punishments should remind us that God is slow to anger, instead we think we don't really deserve death. We end up taking God's mercy for granted.

When Should We Get Angry?

It will be impossible to fully understand the severity of Yahweh's anger, but hopefully this chapter helps us understand why Yahweh got angry and how his anger made sense in the context of the Old Testament. Can we, however, use the God of the Old Testament as a model for appropriate anger in our own context? I think we can, and reviewing the two main types of situations in which Yahweh gets angry will show us why.

First, Yahweh gets angry about a breakdown in relationship. As we saw above with Uzzah and the Israelites at Sinai, Yahweh gets mad when his people break the covenant with him. While this reason might not immediately make sense, when it is put in the context of a marriage, it becomes more reasonable. Most people would say it is legitimate to become angry over an adulterous spouse. Individuals should get angry when a spouse is unfaithful, because the marriage relationship is meant to be exclusive. Many things are meant to be shared, but not husbands and wives. If your spouse is committing adultery, you will be angry if you care about the breakdown in relationship.

Yahweh cares enough about his covenant with his people to get angry when they break it. Similarly, we should care enough about broken relationships with spouses, family members or friends to become upset and even angry when there's a problem. Because of bitterness, hurt or simply apathy, it is easy to ignore or avoid relational problems. Fortunately, Yahweh doesn't take that path but shows us how to value reconciliation.

Anger is often the first step in the reconciliation process. The story of Joseph is often held up as an Old Testament paradigm of family reconciliation, but interestingly, when Joseph first sees his brothers, he yells at them, treats them harshly and throws them into jail for three days (Gen 42:7-17). If we are tempted to sugarcoat Joseph's motivation here not as anger but as something more noble in light of what he says later (Gen 50:20), recall that his brothers were responsible for his thirteen years of slavery and imprisonment (and you thought your brothers were bad). It would be bizarre not to assume Joseph was seriously upset with his brothers for what they did to him.

He was angry not only because he was hurt but also because he cared about the relationship. Joseph's anger served as a catalyst for reconciliation by prompting Reuben to acknowledge that what he and his brothers did to Joseph was wrong (Gen 42:22). Only after Joseph overheard Reuben's confession did he weep (Gen 42:24). The process eventually culminated in the final reconciliation between Joseph and his brothers (Gen 45:1-15; 50:15-21). The examples of Yahweh and Joseph teach us that anger is often an important first step toward forgiveness.

Second, Yahweh gets angry about injustice. His anger about oppression led him first to deliver Israel from Egypt and then to give his people the command to care for widows, orphans and aliens. Yahweh's anger over injustice is a major theme of prophetic literature, particularly Amos. While it seems like most of the time our world doesn't care about injustice or oppression, and certainly wouldn't get mad about it, many influential advocates for the poor have been people of faith, both throughout history (Saint Francis, John Wesley, William Wilberforce) and in recent times (Mother Teresa, Martin Luther King Jr., Jim Wallis, Ron Sider, Bono). All these individuals were influenced by the teachings of both testaments. From the Old Testament specifically, we learn that Yahweh cares enough for the poor and the oppressed to get angry about a lack of compassion. In his anger he even punishes people who oppress others.

Is the God of the Old Testament angry? Yes. Is the God of the Old Testament loving? Yes. Is the God of the New Testament angry? Yes. Is the God of the New Testament loving? Yes. Anger and love are not mutually exclusive. Love for people can lead to anger over a broken relationship. Love for people can also lead to anger about injustice. The God of the Old Testament and New Testament is both quick to love and slow to anger (Jas 1:19). And we should be too.

3

SEXIST OR AFFIRMING?

Atheists and secular feminists state unequivocally that God and the Bible are sexist and therefore are responsible for the loathing of women for the past two thousand years:

> From a barbaric Bronze Age text known as the Old Testament, three anti-human religions have evolved—Judaism, Christianity, and Islam. . . . They are literally, patriarchal—God is the Omnipotent Father—hence the loathing of women for 2,000 years.[1]

> Any honest, thinking person reading through the bible cannot ignore the blatant misogyny and barbarity toward women.[2]

> The place where God's absurdity becomes completely clear is when you look at God's sexism.[3]

Many Christians, however, reply that God and the Bible are not sexist at all:

> The charge of sexism in the Bible is based upon a lack of knowledge of Scripture.[4]

The Bible gives us a lot of proof that God is not sexist.[5]

The Bible does not condone discrimination in any manner.[6]

And feeling torn in the middle are certain women (and sometimes men) in the church who resonate deeply with the first group but feel guilty about not agreeing with the second group.

So, is God and the Old Testament sexist or not?

I would like to side with the Christians who defend the Bible against charges of sexism, but their arguments can sound superficial, like they are shocked anyone could ever say such a thing about the Bible.[7] I wonder if they have ever sat down and listened to someone who is a feminist, particularly one who decided she could no longer be a Christian because of what she read in her Bible about a God who seems sexist. The three quotes from Christians suggest that anyone who accuses the Bible of sexism is either ignorant or illogical. If I were a secular feminist, these statements by Christians would offend me.

I don't think that God or the Bible is sexist, but this is a problem that cannot be easily brushed aside. Many Old Testament texts appear sexist. And sexism is not only a problem in the Bible; it is also a problem in the church. In the summer of 2010, author Anne Rice publicly stated that because of sexism within the church, she no longer considers herself a Christian.[8] Many Christian women feel overlooked, slighted and disempowered within the church, which is tragic, particularly when one realizes that Yahweh and Jesus were both highly affirming of women.

Both the secular feminists and Christians focus on certain biblical texts to defend their positions and then ignore passages that undermine their positions, but if I were to examine all the relevant biblical evidence, it would take more than one chapter.

So I will look only at a few key passages, both ones that suggest that Yahweh is anti-women and others that suggest he is pro-women.[9] The first three chapters of Genesis are mentioned frequently in these discussions, Genesis 1 by the-Bible-is-*not*-sexist camp, Genesis 3 by the-Bible-*is*-sexist camp and Genesis 2 by both camps. So, let's begin in the beginning.[10]

Women Are Godlike

Recently I asked one of my classes, "What is the first thing that comes to mind when you hear Genesis and the first woman?" The first four answers given were "sin," "Eve," "apple" and "serpent."[11] Interestingly, these initial answers portray the woman highly unfavorably, since they focus on Genesis 3, when the serpent tempted her to sin by eating the fruit. (It probably wasn't an apple— they'll need to fix all those paintings—but perhaps a fig, since their clothes came from fig leaves.)

However, we are introduced to the first woman earlier in the text. While the Genesis 3 portrayal of the woman is negative, Genesis 1 and 2 are much more favorable toward women. The first thing the Bible says about women is actually amazingly positive. It is hard to imagine something that could make women look better.

The Bible first tells us that women are made in the image of God:

> Then **God** said, "Let us make humankind[12] in our *image*, according to our *likeness*; and let them have dominion over the fish of the sea, and over the birds of the air, and over the cattle, and over all the wild animals of the earth, and over every creeping thing that creeps upon the earth."
>
> So **God** created humankind in his *image*,

in the *image* of God he created them;
male and female he created them.

God blessed them, and God said to them, "Be fruitful
and multiply, and fill the earth and subdue it; and have
dominion over the fish of the sea and over the birds of the
air and over every living thing that moves upon the earth."
(Gen 1:26-28 NRSV)

Four times in two verses the text states that the humans
were made in God's *image* or *likeness*. (The Hebrew word for
"image," *tselem*, could also be translated as "likeness.") This
four-fold repetition of image/likeness in just two verses tells us
that this idea is important. The first thing that God says about
women is that they are like him. Women are Godlike. (Men are
also Godlike, but most men think that already.)[13] Women are
created by God to be a reflection of himself and his glory. How
are humans to reflect God's image?[14] The fact that God primarily creates in Genesis 1 suggests that the divine-image bearers
are meant to create like he did. As humans fulfill the divine mandate to reproduce, women will play a vital role in the process.[15]

It is significant that the first thing the Bible says about women
is extremely favorable. At least in the beginning, the God of the
Old Testament is highly affirming of women. God thinks that
women are "divine." The idea that women are like God reap-
pears in the next chapter of Genesis.

Woman, the Second Draft

Some people might argue that since the woman was made second she is inferior to the man. That does sound sexist. But often
things that come second are an improvement on what came
before, and as we examine the creation of the woman, we may
be surprised how favorably the "second gender" is portrayed.[16]

Then the LORD God said, "It is not good that the man should be alone; I will make him a *helper fit for him.*" Now out of the ground the LORD God had formed every beast of the field and every bird of the heavens and brought them to the man to see what he would call them. And whatever the man called every living creature, that was its name. The man gave names to all livestock and to the birds of the heavens and to every beast of the field. But for Adam there was not found a *helper fit for him.* So the LORD God caused a deep sleep to fall upon the man, and while he slept took one of his ribs and closed up its place with flesh. And the rib that the LORD God had taken from the man he made into a *woman* and brought her to the man. Then the man said,

"This at last is bone of my bones
    and flesh of my flesh;
she shall be called **Woman,**
    because she was taken out of Man." (Gen 2:18-23)

So Yahweh made the man first and then the woman. To use a writing analogy, the man was the first draft and the woman the second draft. Typically, the second draft of something is better than the first draft. (If you think this version of the book is bad, you should have read the first draft.) Therefore, we could argue that the woman—the second draft—was an improvement on the man—the first draft. We might think that a draft analogy isn't appropriate for the Bible, but if you were to ask most Christians what is more important, the Old Testament or the New Testament, we know what they would say. The one that came later is superior. Genesis 1 also supports this idea, since the humans were created last and on the sixth day after God had created everything else (plants, animals, sun, moon and so on), as the pinnacle or crown jewel of his creation. So, are women superior to men because they came later?

Well, I don't actually think that we should argue for the superiority of women because they, like the New Testament, came second, but I do think that an argument for their inferiority based on Genesis 2 is also invalid.[17]

The accusation of sexism could also be levied against the description of the woman as a "helper" for the man. It could sound like the man, like a traditional businessman, needed a secretary. Therefore, the divinely appointed helper would be like a servant or slave to assist him in his important tasks (cook his meals, iron his shirts, bring his newspaper). Now, that sounds sexist . . . until we look at how the Hebrew word *ezer*, "helper," is used elsewhere in the Old Testament.

Consistently, the one doing the helping is God. With only one exception, at every other time when *ezer* is used in the Pentateuch (the first five Old Testament books) God is the helper (Gen 49:25; Ex 18:4; Deut 33:7, 26, 29).[18] Elsewhere in the Old Testament, and particularly in Psalms and Isaiah, God primarily is the *ezer*, the one who helps his people.[19]

So, instead of being a subservient helper in an inferior position, the woman in Genesis 2 is acting like God for the man to help him, to be his *ezer*. Once again, women are Godlike. In Genesis 1 both men and women are Godlike, but here in Genesis 2 it is just the woman who is acting like God. I don't think Genesis 2 is suggesting that women are superior to men, but it certainly isn't saying they are inferior.

What does it mean that the helper is "suitable" for the man? The Hebrew word *kenegdo* translated as "suitable," literally means "like opposite him," almost a mirror image. There is a connotation of difference as well as sameness, but nothing suggesting inferiority of either gender. The helper is, therefore, not a pawn but a partner, not a flunky but a friend, not a slave but a soul mate.

Genesis is painting a highly favorable image of women—one that would have been shockingly progressive within its ancient Near Eastern context. After two chapters of Genesis, we haven't found anything sexist about God in the Old Testament yet.

When Naked, Husbands Stay Close to Their Wives

A *Non Sequitur* comic strip from 2007 (October 17) depicts the Garden of Eden. The first man explains to his wife about the guy in the background taking notes and wearing clothes (the two of them are, of course, naked): "That's just my publicist. I hired him to make sure the media get the story right. Hey, you should try one of these." He then hands her an apple. There are a half-dozen apple cores at his feet.

Apart from her hiring a publicist, can the portrayal of the woman be redeemed in Genesis 3?

> Now the serpent was more crafty than any other beast of the field that the LORD God had made.
>
> He said to the *woman*, "Did God actually say, 'You shall not eat of any tree in the garden'?" And the woman said to the serpent, "We may eat of the fruit of the trees in the garden, but God said, 'You shall not eat of the fruit of the tree that is in the midst of the garden, neither shall you touch it, lest you die.'" But the serpent said to the *woman*, "You will not surely die. For God knows that when you eat of it your eyes will be opened, and you will be like God, knowing good and evil." So when the *woman* saw that the tree was good for food, and that it was a delight to the eyes, and that the tree was to be desired to make one wise,

she took of its fruit and ate, and she also gave some to her
husband who was with her, and he ate. (Gen 3:1-6)

The story does make the woman look bad. She should not
have listened to the serpent. She should not have eaten the fruit.
She should not have given it to her husband. What she did was
perhaps the worst thing one could possibly imagine.

So is Genesis 3 sexist? I don't think so. If the woman was portrayed negatively and the man positively, we could reasonably
argue that the chapter establishes a precedent for biblical sexism.
However, the man also appears really bad here, and as bad as the
woman's sin was, it appears that the man's sin was worse.

First, he also ate the fruit, but unlike the woman, he didn't
offer any resistance (typical male, always hungry). He was totally passive. Second, he heard the prohibition directly from
Yahweh, but she was dependent on him to deliver the message.
It appears that the message became garbled in transmission
(typical male, doesn't communicate well with the wife). Third,
he was with her when she ate the fruit and did nothing to stop
her, a fact that is often ignored when this passage is taught.
When the serpent speaks here, he uses second person *plural*
forms (basically, "you all"), which don't come across in English
translations, providing further evidence that the man was present for this dialogue and not in another part of the garden.

Whenever I teach Genesis 3, students are shocked to read
that the man was standing next to the woman when she ate. But
we shouldn't be surprised, because at the end of Genesis 2 they
are left clinging to each other as one flesh, and they are both
nude. When naked, husbands stay close to their wives.

Paul, who is accused unfairly of being misogynistic, doesn't
blame the woman, but states that "sin came into the world
through one man" (Rom 5:12).[20] Ultimately, I don't think either

was more at fault, and quibbling about who was more to blame usually doesn't help a problem (except, of course, in marital disputes). They both sinned and both look bad here. So far, I still see no evidence of sexism.

The Curse and the Promise
What about the curse to the woman?

The LORD God *said to the serpent,*

"Because you have done this,
 cursed are you above all livestock
 and above all beasts of the field;
on your belly you shall go,
 and dust you shall eat
 all the days of your life.
I will put enmity between you and the woman,
 and between your offspring and her offspring;
he shall bruise your head,
 and you shall bruise his heel."

To the woman he said,

"I will surely multiply your pain in childbearing;
 in pain you shall bring forth children.
Your desire shall be for your husband,
 and *he shall rule over you.*"

And to Adam he said,

"Because you have listened to the voice of your wife
 and have eaten of the tree
of which I commanded you,
 'You shall not eat of it,'
cursed is the ground because of you;

> in pain you shall eat of it all the days of your life;
> thorns and thistles it shall bring forth for you;
>   and you shall eat the plants of the field.
> By the sweat of your face
>   you shall eat bread,
> till you return to the ground,
>   for out of it you were taken;
> for you are dust,
>   and to dust you shall return." (Gen 3:14-19)

If there is one verse that people who think the Old Testament is sexist focus most on, it would have to be the end of the curse to the woman, specifically that the man will "rule over" her. This verse sounds like a divine mandate for the oppression of females by males. However, as we read the curse to the woman in the context of the other curses, it no longer appears to be anti-women for several reasons.

First, the curse to the woman does not support the oppression of women by men. Literally, the curses are applicable only to the first man and first woman (and first serpent?). Each curse is addressed only to the one intended recipient and the second-person pronouns (*you, your*) are all singular. In other words, God doesn't explicitly address women and men generally here, but only "Adam" and "Eve." Most interpreters, however, reasonably assume that the respective curses carry on to future generations of males and females. I think that is a valid assumption to make, but before doing so we need to acknowledge that an interpretive leap is required to make the curse go beyond the first humans.

The curse still doesn't mean men should oppress women, but simply that a husband will "rule over" his wife. (I realize this sounds sexist, but wait, there's more coming.) So, this curse applies only to married women and not to women in general as a gender. Even though our society believes that those who rule are superior, we need to be careful not to associate inferior status to the one who is being ruled over. In Exodus, Yahweh allowed his chosen people to be ruled over by Egypt for hundreds of years. In the Gospels, Jesus stated that greatness comes not from ruling over others but from serving others (Mk 10:42-45). While Paul tells wives to submit to their husbands, he also speaks of mutual submission (Eph 5:21-22). So, this curse speaks of submission but not oppression, and biblically women are not the only ones who need to submit. God's people in both testaments are called to be submissive.

Second, the man's curse was more severe than the woman's. Her "curse" actually never mentions a curse, while the ground of the man is cursed (and the serpent is directly cursed). She receives more pain in childbirth, but he receives death, returning to the dust.[21] Her pain is limited to the birth process, but his pain endures "all the days of his life."[22] His curse is also almost four times longer than the woman's curse. In the Hebrew, her curse is thirteen words and his is forty-six words. Biblically, there is a correlation between the seriousness of the sin and the length of the judgment.

Third, in the midst of the curses, the woman receives an important promise while the man receives nothing positive. The only hopeful word for the humans here involves a prophecy that the woman's seed will eventually strike the heel of the serpent. It is impossible to overstate the significance of this prediction. It is sometimes called the *protoevangelium*, or the first messianic prophecy, since it is understood traditionally to foreshadow Jesus and his defeat of death on the cross.[23] While this promised victory over the serpent could have mentioned the seed of the man, since they were obviously joint parents, God chooses to focus the blessing on the woman. Perhaps the only other Old Testament promise that rivals this one in significance is the Davidic Promise (2 Sam 7:13-16) that guarantees that David's descendants will rule "forever."

The curse on the woman and the curse on the man were not the same, but that doesn't mean that God was treating the woman in a sexist manner. Unlike curses on the man and the serpent, the woman's "curse" never actually mentions a "curse." Her punishment speaks of submission, not oppression. It was not as severe as the man's curse. And, most significantly, in the midst of these curses, she alone is blessed with a promise.

Not the Way God Wanted It to Be

So, how are we supposed to understand the consequences of Genesis 3? People might say that male rule is something simply to be accepted because it was instituted by God. That sounds sexist. But we need to remember that Genesis 3 is not the way God wanted it to be. The ideal that God established for men and women was Genesis 1 and 2 in the Garden. God initially made the humans, both male and female, Godlike, as mutual partners. The humans blew it by eating the fruit and therefore had to experience the consequences of Genesis 3, which involved a distortion of the ideal male-female relationship. Acceptance of the consequences can lead to oppression of women and other sexist behaviors, but even within Genesis 3 we see a divine example of not simply accepting the consequences.

Even though he uttered the curses, God's behavior in Genesis 2 and 3 reveals his opposition to their effects. The consequences involved pain and toil, but even before the curses God acted as the first anesthesiologist as he put the man to sleep before removing his rib (Gen 2:21), and after the curses God made the work of the man and the woman easier by creating clothes for them and then helping them get dressed (Gen 3:21). Most significantly, within the curses themselves, God declared how he would ultimately defeat the curses through the offspring of the woman. The negative consequences of the curses aren't meant to be accepted. God himself acted to overcome them.

Epidurals and Combine Harvesters

To people who think that women need to be encouraged to be ruled over by men I ask, how do you feel about epidurals and combine harvesters? Most people perceive these modern innovations as good things, even though they diminish the effects of the curse by reducing pain at childbirth and by reducing toil for farmers. It would be bizarre to suggest that we should do nothing to make birth or farming easier based on Genesis 3.

Just as God resists the consequences, we also attempt to diminish their effects. We reduce pain at childbirth. We make it easier to harvest crops. We work to reconcile men and women and to eliminate sexism. With God's help, we are not willing to live in the reality of Genesis 3 (men ruling over women), but we strive to get back to Genesis 1 and 2 (male and female as Godlike helpers for each other), and we look forward to a time when, because of our unity in Christ, distinctions between male and female are diminished (Gal 3:28). The curses are not good things to be welcomed or even unavoidable realities to be accepted but are negative consequences to be overcome.

The book of Genesis teaches important lessons about the relationship between humans and God, and between men and women. Men and women are both divine image-bearers. Men and women are meant to be partners in marriage. Despite being Godlike, both men and women are prone to sin. Even in the context of a passage that appears to be sexist, women are uniquely affirmed. As we examine other texts that address the topic of sexism, we need to understand them in the light of these founda-

tional truths from the first three chapters of the Bible. Later in
Genesis, we find a story that appears to condone the sexual oppression of two young females, so let's turn there next.

Lot and His Daughters

Yahweh decides to judge the city of Sodom for its wickedness,
and after Abraham pleads for the city because his nephew Lot
and his family live there, Yahweh sends two angels who appear
as men (so no wings or halos) to convince Lot to leave town
(Gen 18–19). Lot, being a hospitable guy, persuades the two
strangers not to spend the night in the town square. The men of
Sodom want to show a different kind of hospitality. They are
determined to have the two men join them for a gang rape:

> And they called to Lot, "Where are the men who came to
> you tonight? Bring them out to us, that we may know
> them." Lot went out to the men at the entrance, shut the
> door after him, and said, "I beg you, my brothers, do not
> act so wickedly. Behold, I have two daughters who have
> not known any man. Let me bring them out to you, and do
> to them as you please. Only do nothing to these men, for
> they have come under the shelter of my roof." But they
> said, "Stand back!" And they said, "This fellow came to
> sojourn, and he has become the judge! Now we will deal
> worse with you than with them." Then they pressed hard
> against the man Lot, and drew near to break the door
> down. But the men reached out their hands and brought
> Lot into the house with them and shut the door. And they
> struck with blindness the men who were at the entrance
> of the house, both small and great, so that they wore
> themselves out groping for the door. (Gen 19:5-11)

To protect the two angels and to appease the angry mob, Lot

suggests that the men of Sodom take his daughters instead. It is hard to imagine a father proposing such an evil thing for his daughters. While we didn't find anything sexist in Genesis 1–3, Lot's plan definitely is. His behavior sends a clear message that his two daughters were less valuable than the two strangers. If the narrative were to condone Lot's behavior, then not only is Lot sexist, but Yahweh and the Old Testament are sexist also.

However, I see three reasons to conclude that the narrative is not endorsing Lot's behavior. First, the text here never affirms Lot.[24] An absence of condemnation does not constitute an affirmation. Lot and his family are consistently held up as negative examples in this section of Genesis. He was slow to leave town, his wife disobeyed by rubber-necking to see the carnage, and his daughters intoxicated him and seduced him so they could be impregnated. Lot wasn't rescued because of his righteous behavior but simply because Yahweh was merciful to him, based on the intercession of his uncle Abraham (Gen 18:23-32).

Second, the two angels sent from Yahweh acted in a dramatic way to protect Lot's daughters from the horrific experience that their father proposed. While Yahweh was not an active participant in the narrative, the angels were given supernatural power to prevent the attack. Yahweh and his messengers clearly didn't want the girls to be raped.

Third, the men of the city were punished initially for their attempted rape by being blinded and later for their wicked behavior by having their city destroyed. Yahweh hates rape.[25] This divine animosity toward rape will also be seen as we look at Old Testament laws.

Marrying Your Rapist?

Concentrated within the books of Exodus, Leviticus and Deuteronomy are numerous laws given by Yahweh to the people of Israel on a variety of subjects, including ones touching on issues of gender and sexuality. Several Old Testament laws clearly mandated against rape. In one Old Testament law, rape is considered equivalent to murder, so that the rapist is to be killed and the woman is not punished (Deut 22:25-27). While a death sentence for rape may seem severe, it clearly communicates that rape is evil, that punishment for it will be harsh and that women should be protected from it. Thus the severity of this Old Testament law provides a stronger disincentive for potential rapists than modern, more lenient sentences for rape. Tragically, many rapists probably went unpunished in Israel, as they still do today.

However, other laws about rape may seem sexist. One law states that after a woman who is not engaged has been raped, she is to become the wife of her rapist (Deut 22:28-29). Why would Yahweh give such an apparently sexist command?

To understand why this command was given, we need some cultural background. As evil as rape is today, it was worse in the world of the Old Testament. An unmarried rape victim would not only have to deal with the trauma of the violent act itself, but she would also be stigmatized by the loss of her virginity. Because of her shame, she would be unable to marry. Since the primary way women achieved security then was through marriage, a rape victim could end up impoverished. The world of the Old Testament was more sexist than ours.

This law that appears sexist to us is actually attempting to correct a problem in the sexist world of the Old Testament. While it might not make sense from our perspective, in that context it was a good thing for the victim. The marriage that the law commanded provided the necessary security for the victimized woman and reduced the tragic consequences of the rape. The law also commanded that the man is never permitted to divorce her, so a woman who has been raped has a guarantee of future security that most women would not have. The man must also pay the bride dowry, giving the union the appearance of a normal marriage.

More Evil Than Rape?

An example from David's family helps us understand the context of this rape law from Deuteronomy. When Tamar was raped by her half-brother Amnon (2 Sam 13:1-20), even though beforehand she begged him not to rape her, afterward she begged him not to send her away. She even told Amnon that sending her away would be more evil than the rape itself. (Amnon still forced her to leave, and despite her beauty, Tamar never remarried.)[26] While her comment to Amnon is shocking to us, her perspective is consistent with the rape law from Deuteronomy. A victimized woman did not think it was sexist to marry her rapist.

Our hasty conclusion that Yahweh's command here is sexist reveals an ignorance of their culture. As the story of Tamar shows, a woman victimized by rape in that context would view the marriage as necessary. A law commanding the marriage of a rapist and his victim is inconceivable today, but in the time of Tamar, it was a good thing for the woman. By giving the command, God was not being sexist, but rather was combating the sexism of the culture.

As we examine other Old Testament laws concerning women, we can find other laws that appear sexist from our twenty-first-century context. However, as William Webb argues, laws in the Old Testament concerning women consistently move in a redemptive direction in comparison to parallel laws from its ancient Near Eastern context.[27] From our perspective, they appear sexist, but within their own context they were progressive. For example, Assyrian laws concerning theft proscribe harsher penalties for women than men (usually death), while the parallel Old

Testament laws make no distinctions between the penalties for men and women (Ex 22:1-4; Lev 19:11, 13).[28] As we move beyond laws to discuss a few impressive biblical women, we see more evidence that the God of the Old Testament affirms women.

A Female "President" and Three Female Advisers

Recent research reported in the London *Times* claims that the "Bible's negative stance on women is a myth," concluding that most biblical women are portrayed either positively or neutrally, with four times as many female "saints" as "sinners."[29] We might look at the results of these types of studies with suspicion, but the fact remains that, with the blessing of Yahweh, women did some amazing things in the world of the Old Testament. While most progressive democracies in the world today have never been ruled by a woman, Yahweh selected a female "president" (Deborah; Judg 4) over three millennia ago (and people say Yahweh is sexist?). Deborah was not only the political leader of Israel, but as the prophet of Yahweh she was also the spiritual leader of the nation (so basically "president" and "pope"). Deborah also composed a poem that is recorded in the Bible, as did Hannah and Mary the mother of Jesus.[30] If it is okay for women to compose sections of the Bible, perhaps we should let them teach it?

In the books of 1 and 2 Samuel, three wise women confronted male leaders of their nation and promoted peace in the process. Abigail risked her life in an attempt to persuade David not to slaughter the household of Nabal, so David relented, commenting that Yahweh had sent Abigail to him to prevent bloodshed (1 Sam 25). The wise woman of Tekoa convinced David to become reconciled to Absalom (2 Sam 13). The wise woman of Abel persuaded Joab, David's military commander, to cease his siege of the city after the people of Abel kill the rebel Sheba (2 Sam 20:14-22). Yahweh used these three wise women to advise a king and his commander. We can't accuse David and Joab of being wimps or not masculine because they were influenced by women—they were two of the biggest military heroes in Israel's history. Real men learn from women. Wise men like David and Joab listen to wise women.

While readers of the Old Testament may not be familiar with the stories of Deborah and Abigail, most are familiar with the stories of two other heroic Old Testament women, Ruth and Esther. Ruth was a widow who gave up her homeland of Moab to take care of another widow, her Israelite mother-in-law, Naomi. She worked hard as a gleaner in the fields of Boaz, she committed herself to the God of Israel, and she was blessed to be an ancestor of David and Jesus. Esther, because of her beauty, was selected as queen of Persia, but when her people the Jews were in danger, she risked her life for her country. These two women were honored by men and by Yahweh, and the two Old Testament books named after them are devoted to their stories. As we shift to the New Testament we'll discover that, not surprisingly, Jesus also affirmed women.

Anointing the Anointed One

In Jesus' day, men did not speak to women in public (Jn 4:27), but Jesus consistently took women seriously. He interacted with women,[31] he told stories in which a woman was the hero,[32] and he generously affirmed women. Jesus didn't actually affirm people very often (he frequently rebuked people, though), so when he affirmed someone, it was significant. Martha was taking the traditional woman's role preparing food, but Jesus affirmed Mary's decision to act like a man and sit at the feet of the rabbi to learn (Lk 10:38-42). Rich people were giving massive quantities of cash to the temple, but Jesus affirmed a poor widow who gave everything she had (Mk 12:43-44). Perhaps the individual that Jesus affirmed most dramatically in the Gospels was a woman:

> And while **he** [Jesus] was at Bethany in the house of Simon the leper, as **he** was reclining at table, a *woman* came with an alabaster flask of ointment of pure nard, very costly, and she broke the flask and poured it over **his** head. There were some who said to themselves indignantly, "Why was the ointment wasted like that? For this ointment could have been sold for more than three hundred denarii and given to the poor." And they scolded *her*. But **Jesus** said, "Leave *her* alone. Why do you trouble *her*? *She* has done a beautiful thing to me. For you always have the poor with you, and whenever you want, you can do good for them. But you will not always have me. *She* has done what *she* could; *she* has anointed my body beforehand for burial. And truly, I say to you, wherever the gospel is proclaimed in the whole world, what *she* has done will be told in memory of *her*." (Mk 14:3-9)

This unnamed woman performs an incredible act of generosity and humility. In today's currency, the ointment she dumped over Jesus' head was worth at least thirty thousand dollars.[33] The behavior of this woman is even more shocking when set in contrast to what all the men around Jesus were doing. The chief priests were plotting to kill Jesus (Mk 14:1), Judas was planning to betray Jesus (Mk 14:10), the disciples were about to desert Jesus (Mk 14:27), and Peter was about to deny him (Mk 14:66-72). Religious leaders and Jesus' closest friends were all hurting him, but this woman was blessing him.

She apparently understood concepts that the disciples had trouble with. She seemed to comprehend that Jesus was the Christ, or "the anointed one." What do you do to the anointed one? Anoint him. The disciples,[34] however, didn't think the anointed one should be anointed, so they rebuked her for anointing him. When she made no reply to their rebuke, Jesus came to her defense and rebuked them for rebuking her. He thought her action was beautiful, not wasteful.

Jesus also suggested that she understood that he needed to die, since she was preparing his body for burial. The disciples repeatedly had problems understanding that Jesus' path would soon lead to death, but this woman seemed to have figured it out.

Jesus declared to the men that followed him that her deed would be immortalized along with the gospel. He predicted that she would be affirmed all over the world for her act. Not only was her act extravagant, but Jesus' affirmation of her was also extravagant. No other individual in the Gospels received this level of praise from Jesus.

The disciples of Jesus just didn't get it. They didn't understand that Jesus, like Yahweh, affirmed women. Unfortunately, many disciples of Jesus today still have the same problem. Instead of following Jesus' example of praising women who want to serve, we are often more like the sexist disciples, rebuking women who take initiative.

Why Do People Think the Old Testament God Is Sexist?

In the sexist context of the Old Testament and New Testament, Yahweh and Jesus both affirmed women. So why do people think the God of the Old Testament is sexist? While this question is hard to answer, instead of blaming the Old Testament, other factors need to be examined. Sexism in society and the church contribute significantly to the problem. Yahweh and Jesus were progressive within their context in honoring women, but often the church is not. While I might have a hard time changing a sexist society and only a slightly easier time changing sexism in the church, I can do something about my own sexist tendencies. Here are three suggestions I've tried to implement.

First, since women are made in the image of God, listen to women and learn about God from them. Wise men like David are willing to listen to wise women. I've committed myself to read about and study the lives of godly women in the Bible, like Abigail and Deborah. I also read female contemporary authors. Women often have no problem reading male authors, but men tend to avoid female authors. Military heroes like David and Joab didn't think their masculinity was somehow compromised by learning from females. A humble male should be able to learn from men and women.

Second, follow the example of Yahweh and Jesus, and affirm women whenever possible. When teaching, I try to use positive examples of women from the Bible, church history and recent history. I fulfill Jesus' prophecy whenever I teach on the woman who anointed him. (Go ahead, you can fulfill the prophecy too.) When a woman speaks up in one of my classes, I try to refer back to her insights in a positive manner. Publicly, I refrain from making derogatory comments about women and only speak positively about my wife.

Third, talk (and write) about sexism. Gender issues are huge in contemporary culture, but not in the church (we, like the disciples, just don't get it). When a woman brings up the topic of sexism in church, people often think she is doing it to promote a hidden agenda.[35] If she does it with an edge, people simply ignore her because she is perceived as having an ax to grind. Men need to bring up the subject more often, and not because it is politically correct, but because it is biblically correct. Both Yahweh and Jesus promoted, empowered and affirmed women.

Men Behaving Badly

My wife, Shannon, and I were on staff together with InterVarsity for the first eight years of our marriage. We moved three times during that period, and each time we would visit numerous churches to discern where we should worship. Frequently, when we would visit a new church, we would introduce ourselves to the pastor, affirm him (almost never "her") for the sermon and then tell him about our ministry to college students. He would then turn to face me, ask me questions and basically ignore Shannon.

I initially found this behavior bizarre, but it happened so regularly, I started to interject, "My wife, Shannon, is also on staff. She's is a gifted teacher, a creative minister and loves students." He would briefly acknowledge my comment ("Oh, that's nice.") and then shift the focus of the conversation back to me or the church. While I appreciated his interest in me, I would be frustrated by his lack of interest in my wife and her ministry. Shannon would always leave these interactions feeling disempowered and devalued. She and I are already committed to being involved in a local church, but my fear is that this type of experience is repeated on Sunday mornings in many churches around the world and, since first impressions are so important, many women won't be coming back.

But it doesn't need to be like this. Wouldn't it be great if both men and women were regularly welcomed and affirmed by people in positions of leadership in the church? I realize that some male pastors might feel uncomfortable speaking with a female in certain contexts, but they are going to need to find appropriate ways to move beyond that feeling if they want to affirm and empower women like Yahweh and Jesus did.

In our culture and in the church, men are on the top of the totem pole. If you are on top, why would you voluntarily help to lift up others? Because Jesus told us that serving others is the way to be great, and he modeled it himself. As more readers and teachers of the Bible emphasize that God affirms women, our culture will realize that Yahweh isn't sexist. I hope even women who have been victims of sexism will see God not only as the one who created them in his image but also as the one who desires relationship with them.

4

RACIST OR HOSPITABLE?

"Well, for once the rich white man is in control."

Charles Montgomery Burns, owner of the Springfield Nuclear Power Plant, makes this statement in *The Simpsons Movie* (2007), after the city of Springfield asks for his help getting desperately needed power. According to Burns, poor, minority females are the real power brokers in the world. He probably needs to get out more often.

There's a popular perception that the God of the Old Testament, perhaps like Burns, is out of touch when it comes to issues of race. Over thirty-five years ago, William R. Jones wrote a book titled *Is God a White Racist?*[1] The British pop singer and songwriter Lily Allen asks in her 2009 single "Him" about God, "Do you think his favorite type of human is Caucasian?"[2] Richard Dawkins doesn't ask a question, but states categorically that the God of the Old Testament is racist (and misogynistic, megalomaniacal, sadomasochistic and so on).[3]

Why Does Yahweh Seem Racist?

Why do people think that Yahweh is racist? There are many reasons, but two stand out. *First,* nineteenth-century Christians used Old Testament texts to support slavery based on race, which could suggest that the God of the Old Testament condones racial discrimination. *Second*, Yahweh commanded the Israelites to kill all the Canaanites, which sounds like a divine mandate for genocide. This chapter will, therefore, discuss Old Testament passages concerning slavery and the Canaanites, as well as laws about foreigners and a story of the healing of a foreign terrorist.

Before working through passages, we need to be clear about definitions. If we define racism simply as prejudice based on distinctions among the primary races (for example, European, African, Asian), it would be hard to find obvious examples of racism in the Old Testament, since almost everyone there is of the same basic racial stock. They would not have looked as different as a northern European does from a southern African or from an eastern Asian. However, if we broaden the definition to include prejudice based on nationality or ethnicity, we find numerous Old Testament texts that could appear racist. Typically, the Old Testament will address the issue of race by referring to non-Israelites as foreigners, aliens or sojourners, so I will focus on texts that mention these groups.

In the previous chapter we began "in the beginning" of the Old Testament, and Genesis lays the foundation for a biblical understanding not only about gender but also about race. God created man and woman in the image of God and then commanded them to multiply and fill the earth (Gen 1:26-28), and over time groups of peoples and nations were eventually created, all of which reflect the divine image. Attitudes that denigrate people of a particular race are, therefore, not only racist but also insulting to the God who created all people in his image. Racism ultimately is blasphemous, since the Bible first informs us that the people of each and every ethnicity resemble

God himself. Genesis has still more to teach us about race.

We Are Family

What part of the Bible do people skip over most frequently? Without a doubt it has to be genealogies. I have yet to find a poster with a beautiful waterfall cascading down a valley with these words:

> When Arpachshad had lived thirty-five years he begat Shelah, and Arpachshad lived after the birth of Shelah four hundred three years and had other sons and daughters.[4]

The biblical authors, however, don't share our aversion to detailed family histories. A significant portion of the beginning of Genesis is genealogy (all of Gen 5 and Gen 10, and much of Gen 4 and Gen 11). As we read the great stories about Abel, Cain, Seth[5] and Noah, the narrative is interrupted by boring lists of names. Why does the Bible waste so much "prime real estate" on genealogy?

Because race is important to God. The main message communicated through these "boring lists of names" is that God is interested in where peoples and nations came from. When it comes to the issue of race, genealogies play an important role at the beginning of both the Old Testament and the New Testament.

The list in Genesis 10 includes the descendants of Noah's three sons, Japheth, Ham and Shem, after God started over with his family following the flood. The chapter concludes by stating that the nations spread all over the earth after the flood. According to Genesis, all nations are ultimately related to each other. We are family.

The fact that everyone is related to each other should undermine any attempt at racial prejudice. Racism is not only insulting to God, but it is also insulting to your own extended family. So far in Genesis, there's nothing to suggest God is racist.

Noah Doesn't Like Ham

After the flood, Noah plants a vineyard (Gen 9:18-27). One night he gets drunk and lies down in his tent naked (as one apparently does in those circumstances). His middle son, Ham, sees him in this condition and informs his two brothers, who quickly and discreetly cover up their father. When Noah realizes what happened, he gets mad at Ham and curses Canaan, Ham's son, by saying that he will always serve Japheth and Shem.

This is a confusing story that raises many questions. Isn't Noah the one to blame for getting drunk and naked? What's so bad about seeing your father naked? Why does Noah not like Ham? (Perhaps it's a kosher thing?) But we won't discuss all these questions, since they aren't directly relevant to the issue of racism. The so-called Ham curse, however, is relevant. It was used by nineteenth-century Christians as a justification for slavery, since Ham's descendants were generally thought to be Africans, while Japheth's descendants were thought to be Europeans.[6] If this justification is valid, then it would appear that Yahweh is, in fact, racist. Fortunately, however, it isn't and he isn't.

This curse should not be used as a justification for slavery for three reasons. First, the bizarreness of the story makes it impossible to draw deeper conclusions about any possible ongoing implications. The curse literally affected only one generation of Noah's sons, so to argue that it somehow carries over into nineteenth-century America is outrageous.

Second, the curse wasn't uttered by Yahweh, but by Noah, and he wasn't exactly a paradigm of piety at this point in his life. (It's tempting to simply blame his grumpy behavior on a nasty hangover.) Despite Noah's state, Yahweh did apparently grant power to the curse, but even so, the curse had a very limited focus, which leads to the next point.

Third, the curse targeted only Canaan and not Ham or all Ham's sons. This is actually the strangest thing about the curse (and being a clever reader, you were probably wondering about it already). Ham's older sons, Cush and Egypt, were more obviously connected to Africa (Cush was Ethiopia and Egypt was . . . Egypt), but Canaan's descendants were related to the people that the Israelites encountered in the land of Canaan (the Amorites, Jebusites, Hivites and all those other people-ites). Egypt actually enslaved Israel before any Canaanite enslavement occured. The curse on Canaan, therefore, foreshadows the conflict between Israel and the Canaanites, which I'll discuss in the next section.

Therefore, the incorrectly named "Ham curse" doesn't justify slavery in any context other than ancient Israel and Canaan. While the Old Testament allowed slavery, William Webb argues persuasively that the biblical attitude on slavery was progressive within its ancient context, moving in a redemptive direction.[7] The fact that Yahweh delivered the Israelites from Egyptian enslavement suggests he doesn't condone the institution. The fact that the Old Testament refers to this deliverance literally hundreds of times tells us that God didn't want them to forget that he hates slavery. The fact that people of African descent were enslaved in the United States cannot, therefore, be blamed on Yahweh, the Old Testament or even Noah, but rather should be blamed exclusively on racism within the United States and on larger global forces that contributed to the transatlantic slave trade.

However, moving from the issue of slavery to genocide, we

can link what happened when Israel entered the Promised Land to the curse on Canaan. Is the Canaanite genocide justified simply because their ancient ancestor had voyeuristic tendencies? That would be harsh, perhaps even racist, so let's go there next.

A Canaanite Genocide?

Perhaps the Old Testament texts that potentially make Yahweh appear the most racist are the ones that describe divinely mandated slaughters of foreigners, specifically the Canaanites. After entering Canaan, Joshua is said to have left no one remaining, after having destroyed all that breathed, as Yahweh had commanded (Josh 10:40; compare Josh 11:14-15). Should the slaughter of the Canaanites by God's people be considered an act of genocide?

Tragically, the issue of ethnic cleansing never seems to go away. The history of the twentieth century includes genocides of Armenians by Turks, Jews by Nazis, Tutsis by Hutus.[8] More recently the slaughter of the Fur people by the Janjawid in Darfur has made headlines. The most pervasive source of global instability today, the tension between Israel and the Palestinians, has its roots in the battles over the land that was once called Canaan. So, a discussion of this most troubling aspect of the Old Testament could shed light on recent acts of ethnic violence and perhaps even on the pervasive conflicts between Muslims and Christians throughout the world.

The Israelite Exiles Needed a Homeland

Before looking at the biblical context of the Canaanite conquest, we first need to understand the ancient context. Typically, after a battle, the victorious army either enslaved the defeated army or wiped it out completely. Ashurnasirpal of Assyria described in graphic detail on one of his temple reliefs how he burned, mutilated and hung captives, including boys and girls, from one of his conquered cities.[9] King Mesha of Moab erected a monument that boasted after a military victory about killing all the inhabitants of two Israelite towns, including women and girls.[10] These descriptions of brutal violence are not unique within the ancient Near East.

The major point of similarity between the biblical conquest narratives and those of their neighbors is the hyperbolic language.[11] The hyperbolic nature of the two Joshua texts can be seen when they are examined alongside other texts. While Joshua 10:40 and Joshua 11:12-15 speak of everyone being destroyed, elsewhere in Joshua and Judges a different perspective is given. These other texts repeatedly state that the Israelites did not kill all the Canaanites; they couldn't even drive all of them out of the land (Josh 13:1-6; 15:63; 17:12; Judg 1:19-34).[12] The book of Joshua even refers to foreigners not just living among the Israelites but also participating in the covenant renewal ceremony (Josh 8:33, 35). To reconcile these two divergent perspectives on Israel's conquest, a nonliteral reading of the texts that speak of "all" people being destroyed is required. Based on the textual evidence, we can conclude that the Israelite conquest was not as severe as the two short passages (Josh 10:40; 11:12-15) might suggest.

While the violent descriptions of the Joshua accounts are still problematic, relative to the conquests of Ashurnasirpal and Mesha, Joshua's victory over the Canaanites was much less excessive. There is no mention of women or children, and no descriptions of brutality or mutilation. In comparison to Ashurnasirpal's graphic details, the Joshua narrative is rather terse concerning the actual bloodshed (Josh 10:40; 11:12-14). Instead of a glorification of brutality found in the Assyrian and Moabite versions, the book of Joshua emphasizes obedience to Yahweh.

The primary difference, however, among these descriptions of violence is that, unlike Assyria and Moab, which were expanding their own borders to enrich their own kingdoms, Israel was simply attempting to gain a homeland. They were refugees who had experienced hundreds of years of oppression in a foreign land and needed a place to live. Since their ancestors—Abraham, Isaac and Jacob—had lived in Canaan previously (Gen 13:12; 16:3; 23:20; 25:10-11; 26:6; 33:18-19; 37:1), they were repossessing land that had belonged to their family, some of which had been purchased from the previous residents (Gen 23:16-18; 25:10; 33:19; 50:13). We could argue that they had a legitimate right to be reestablished in the land of their ancestors.

Promise and Punishment

We can now look at the biblical context of these narratives, observing two factors that help us view the conquest of Israel's homeland less negatively. First, God had repeatedly promised the land to Abraham, Isaac, Jacob and their descendants (for example, Gen 12:7; 15:18-21; 17:8; 26:2-3; 28:13-15; 46:1-4; Ex 3:8; 13:5; 23:31-33; 34:11-16). The consistent repetition of this promise throughout the Pentateuch foreshadows the eventual conquest, preparing the reader for the inevitable battles in Canaan. The gift of the land was one of the primary ways Yahweh planned to bless Israel, and it was through this land that God would work his ultimate purposes to bless and call all nations to himself (1 Kings 4:34; Ps 67:2; Is 2:2-4; 66:18-21; Jer 3:17). If Yahweh were racist, he would only want to bless his own people, but he blessed Israel with land so that all the families of the earth would ultimately be blessed (Gen 12:3).

Second, the destruction of the inhabitants of the land is

viewed as an act of divine punishment against the Canaanites because of their exceeding wickedness (Gen 15:16; Ex 34:13-16; Lev 18:25; Deut 9:5; 20:18), which involved not only idolatry (Ex 23:32-33; Deut 12:29-31), child sacrifice and sorcery (Deut 18:9-14), but also unwarranted attacks on defenseless Israel. After the Israelites were freed from Egyptian enslavement, they were attacked by various groups of Canaanite people: the Amalekites (Ex 17:8-13), Arad (Num 21:1), the Amorites (Num 21:21-26; Deut 2:26-37) and Bashan (Num 21:33-35; Deut 3:1-22).[13] Balak, the king of Moab, also wanted to attack them (Num 22–24) but was thwarted by Balaam and a talking donkey. The Israelites initiated none of these initial engagements because they were a wandering band of unarmed political refugees. The nations that attacked them were taking advantage of Israel's weak situation. The Canaanites were guilty of many crimes, but it is hard not to conclude that the severity of the judgment against them was due in no small part to a lack of hospitality and an abundance of hostility.

While the level of violence of the divine judgment of Joshua may seem excessive, elsewhere in the Old Testament God consistently punished evil nations with death and exile (Amos 1:5, 15; 5:5; Jer 48:7). He even judged his own people as first Israel and then Judah were destroyed and exiled from their land (2 Kings 17; 24–25). If Yahweh were racist, he would punish only other nations, not his own. God granted Israel the land, but he also removed them from the land, despite his promise to them, because they were wicked just like the Canaanites. The reason he did not give the land fully to Abraham earlier is that the iniquity of the inhabitants was "not yet complete" (Gen 15:16). So, even though the residents of Canaan deserved punishment hundreds of years earlier, God was gracious and slow to anger, giving them centuries to repent (see chapter two, "Angry or

Loving?"). Part of our problem with the conquest narratives comes from our discomfort with judgment more generally, but since punishment is found throughout Scripture, we need to continue to work to understand it and see how it fits in with God's mission to bless the nations.

Prostitute Hospitality

To support the idea that Canaanite inhospitality toward Israel contributed to the judgment against them, every Canaanite person or nation that showed mercy to Israel was delivered. Rahab, the prostitute from Jericho, welcomed two spies into her home, so when Joshua fought the battle of Jericho and the walls came tumbling down, she and her entire family were rescued (Josh 6). (Rahab not only became part of the Israelite nation but she also had several famous descendants, see below.) Although the Gibeonites used deception, they still welcomed and fed their new Israelite neighbors and, most significantly, they initiated a peace treaty, so they were all saved (Josh 9). When a man from the city of Bethel helped a different set of Israelite spies, he and his entire family were spared (Judg 1:24-25). After Israel established a monarchy and Saul was told to destroy the Amalekites for attacking defenseless Israel in the wilderness, he specifically told the Kenites who were living among the Amalekites that they would not be destroyed, because they were kind to Israel (1 Sam 15:6). Each of these groups of people who acted hospitably toward Israel was spared from the conquest.

The reason Yahweh judged the people of Canaan was not because he was racist but because they were wicked. Yahweh didn't hate the Canaanites, but he hated the crimes they committed. Yahweh showed mercy to Canaanites who practiced hospitality toward foreigners, even to a prostitute's family. And as we will soon see, he commanded his own people to practice hospitality toward foreigners.

The Canaanite conquest is probably the most problematic topic in the Old Testament, and it will, therefore, be impossible to "solve it" in a few pages. We discussed it already briefly in the anger chapter (two) and will revisit it in the next chapter on violence (five).[14] While I would hope my arguments presented here are helpful, questions certainly will remain. I must resort to taking it on faith that even though God commanded his people to kill the Canaanites, he still loves the nations and ultimately wants to bless them. So, we'll leave the Canaanite problem for now and move to Israel's laws about foreigners.

Love the Sojourner

While Yahweh gave laws that treated foreigners differently than Israelites, these laws legislated relatively minor concerns, mainly keeping Israel separate from their neighbors. Israelites can charge interest only to foreigners (Deut 23:20). Foreigners can't eat the Passover unless they are circumcised (Ex 12:43-48). No foreigner can serve as Israel's king (Deut 17:15). If these were the only laws regarding foreigners that Yahweh gave Israel, we could argue that their "separate but equal" approach smacks of racism (it was certainly racist in U.S. history).

However, Israel had other laws that stood in direct opposition to a "separate but equal" version of racism. They were supposed to treat foreigners just like other Israelites (Lev 24:22; Num 9:14; 15:15-16). And other laws went beyond simply treating foreigners as equals, including this one given by Moses:

> For the LORD your **God** is **God** of gods and Lord of lords,
> the great, the mighty, and the awesome **God**, who is not

partial and takes no bribe. He executes justice for the fatherless and the widow, and *loves* the *sojourner*, giving him food and clothing. *Love* the *sojourner*, therefore, for you were *sojourners* in the land of Egypt. (Deut 10:17-19)

Moses' declaration that Yahweh is not partial is about as close as you will find in the Old Testament to a statement that God isn't racist. But Moses' claim here could even seem defensive, the sort of thing you have to say about someone who actually *is* racist. ("He's not a racist, but he just does all these things that seem racist.") What reasons does Moses give that Yahweh isn't partial, or racist?

First, Yahweh executes justice for the *sojourner*. At this point my sons would say, "Dad, *actually* it only states that he executes justice for orphans and widows." My reply: "Yes, but Moses goes on to explain that he gives food and clothes to sojourners and he delivered them while they were oppressed sojourners in Egypt. That sounds a lot like an execution of justice for sojourners by God." If my sons weren't convinced yet, I would point them to other texts in which God commands Israel not to pervert justice for the sojourner and then he curses those who do just that (Deut 24:17; 27:19).

Second, Yahweh *loves* sojourners. How do we know Yahweh loves foreigners? Practicing justice is certainly an act of love, but Yahweh goes way beyond that. He loves sojourners by commanding his people to love sojourners.[15] And Deuteronomy isn't the only place he gives this command. In Leviticus, he tells them to love the foreigners as they love themselves (Lev 19:34). Yahweh not only gives them commands to love and care for non-Israelites, he also warns them he will punish those who mistreat or oppress foreigners (Ex 22:20-24; 23:9; Lev 19:33; Deut 23:7; 24:14; 27:19; Ezek 22:7, 29; Zech 7:10; Mal 3:5).[16] The psalmist tells us that Yahweh watches over the foreigner (Ps 146:9).

Did Israel always follow these laws? Unfortunately they did not, but Yahweh certainly did encourage and exhort his people to love non-Israelites. He commanded them to practice hospitality toward foreigners and punished them when they didn't.

Healing a Terrorist

Yahweh gave these laws in an attempt to make his people welcome foreigners, but so far we've looked only at examples where they were slaughtering foreigners. The book of Ruth narrates how a woman from Moab, one of Israel's traditional enemies, is brought into the people of God and becomes the great-grandmother of Israel's greatest king, David. The book of Daniel tells the story of how God reveals his power to two foreign emperors, Nebuchadnezzar and Darius, leading each of them to praise him. The book of Jonah describes how God uses a racist Israelite to show his love for the hated Assyrian capital of Nineveh. But since Ruth, Daniel and Jonah are popular stories (and each has a VeggieTales version),[17] let's look in more depth at a less familiar story, involving Naaman the Syrian general.

> Naaman, commander of the army of the king of Syria, was a great man with his master and in high favor, because by him the LORD had given victory to Syria. He was a mighty man of valor, but he was a leper. Now the Syrians on one of their raids had carried off a little girl from the land of Israel, and she worked in the service of Naaman's wife. She said to her mistress, "Would that my lord were with the prophet who is in Samaria! He would cure him of his leprosy." So Naaman went in and told his lord, "Thus and so spoke the girl from the land of Israel.". . .

So Naaman came with his horses and chariots and stood at the door of Elisha's house. And Elisha sent a messenger to him, saying, "Go and wash in the Jordan seven times, and your flesh shall be restored, and you shall be clean." But Naaman was angry and went away, saying, "Behold, I thought that he would surely come out to me and stand and call upon the name of the LORD his God, and wave his hand over the place and cure the leper. Are not Abana and Pharpar, the rivers of Damascus, better than all the waters of Israel? Could I not wash in them and be clean?" So he turned and went away in a rage. But his servants came near and said to him, "My father, it is a great word the prophet has spoken to you; will you not do it? Has he actually said to you, 'Wash, and be clean'?" So he went down and dipped himself seven times in the Jordan, according to the word of the **man of God**, and his flesh was restored like the flesh of a little child, and he was clean. Then he returned to the **man of God**, he and all his company, and he came and stood before him. And he said, "Behold, I know that there is no **God** in all the earth but in Israel." (2 Kings 5:1-4, 9-15)

At this point in Israel's history, their biggest enemy was Syria. The two nations were in the middle of a war that lasted over a century (1 Kings 15:18-20; 2 Kings 13:25). Naaman was the enemy general responsible for Syria's current victories. Not only had he defeated Israel numerous times, but the text also tells us that during his raids he kidnapped Israelite children and made them slaves. Israelites would have viewed Naaman like we view terrorists today; he was the Osama bin Laden of his time.

Next, the story introduces us to yet another female hero. While Naaman was powerful, prestigious and had the favor of the king, this girl was young, foreign and had the status of a slave. The text doesn't even tell us her name. If I were a slave, I might be a bit bitter at my master, particularly if he were the one who captured me and took me away from my family. But this particular slave girl wants her master to be healed of his leprosy and she knows who can do it, Elisha the prophet of Yahweh. To his credit, Naaman is willing to give the foreign prophet a try at healing his leprosy based only on the recommendation of a young slave girl.

Now Elisha enters the narrative. He could have said he would never heal a foreign terrorist, but instead he tells Naaman to get "baptized" in the Jordan, dunking himself seven times. Naaman thinks this is outrageous and makes a racist statement, that the rivers of Damascus (his capital) are better than the river of Israel. But, once again, one of his servants speaks up, suggesting he try Elisha's method. Naaman does it, is healed and then declares that the God of Israel is the only God of all the earth.

God didn't seem to do anything in this story, so what does it have to do with God not being racist? This story actually shows us that God isn't racist for three reasons. First, at the beginning of the story Yahweh gave victory to Syria. While Yahweh frequently helped Israel defeat their enemies, he also frequently allowed his own people to suffer defeat at the hands of their enemies. In the book of Judges, Yahweh punished the Israelites by giving victory to their neighbors (Hazor, Moab, Midian and Philistia). At the end of 2 Kings, Yahweh allowed first Assyria to conquer the Northern Kingdom of Israel and then Babylon to conquer the Southern Kingdom of Judah. We don't know why Syria received divine assistance here, but it's clear that Yahweh helped both Israel and their neighbors in battle.

Second, the people of Yahweh obeyed his command to love the foreigner despite having a legitimate reason not to do so. By informing the man who had enslaved her about Elisha's power, the Israelite slave girl served as the initial catalyst for the healing. She loved the foreigner. By giving directions to the man who had victimized Israel, Elisha completed the healing process. He loved the foreigner.

Third, Yahweh healed a foreign general. Yes, the girl and Elisha played a role in the process, but Yahweh ultimately was the reason for the healing. Elisha had the power to heal only because he was a man of God, and Naaman clearly perceived his healing coming from the God of Israel.

The fact that the story of Naaman is included in the Bible suggests that the authors of the Old Testament wanted to emphasize that God welcomes, heals and loves foreigners. If this story were the only one in the Old Testament in which God loved foreigners, then the argument that God isn't racist would seem to be thinly supported. However, books like Ruth, Daniel and Jonah reveal Yahweh's love for non-Israelites; and Israel's laws commanded the love of foreigners; and genealogies record that loving foreigners is actually loving your own family. Two other prophetic texts describe Yahweh's incredible, but no longer surprising, concern for other nations: Ethiopia, the Philistines and the Arameans in Amos 9:7, and Egypt and Assyria in Isaiah 19:23-25.[18]

As we move on to the New Testament, we'll see that Jesus, just like Yahweh, was a xenophile (foreign-lover).

The Foreign Grandmothers of Jesus
Most readers of the Bible ignore the beginning of the New Testament.

> The book of the genealogy of Jesus Christ, the son of David, the son of Abraham. Abraham was the father of

Isaac, and Isaac the father of Jacob, and Jacob the father of Judah and his brothers, and Judah the father of Perez and Zerah *by Tamar*, and Perez the father of Hezron, and Hezron the father of Ram, and Ram the father of Amminadab, and Amminadab the father of Nahshon, and Nahshon the father of Salmon, and Salmon the father of Boaz *by Rahab*, and Boaz the father of Obed *by Ruth*, and Obed the father of Jesse, and Jesse the father of David the king. And David was the father of Solomon *by the wife of Uriah*. (Mt 1:1-6)

In the midst of this list of names recording the lineage of Jesus, two surprising things stand out.[19] First, the list includes four women. It was unusual in ancient genealogies to include mothers, so we find yet another example of Scripture progressively affirming women (see chapter three). Second, and more to the point of this chapter, the four women all appear to be foreigners. Tamar and Rahab were both Canaanites, Ruth was from Moab, and Bathsheba was probably a Hittite. While these aspects of Jesus' ancestry could have easily been glossed over, since women weren't typically included in genealogies, the initial verses of the New Testament highlight Jesus' foreign ancestry. If God were a racist, he wouldn't welcome foreign women into his family and then have them listed prominently in his son's family tree.

The "Good" American

Before looking at one of Jesus' best-known stories, I want to mention briefly four other places in the Gospels that support the idea that Jesus loves foreigners (I could list many more). In Luke 4, Jesus mentioned another foreign woman, a widow cared for by Elijah, as well as our foreign terrorist friend, Naaman the Syrian who was healed by Elisha. In John 4, Jesus' interaction with yet another impressive foreign woman, a Samaritan, shocked his disciples but transformed her into an evangelist to her entire village. In Mark 7, Jesus healed the daughter of the Syrophoenician woman (we'll discuss this more in chapter seven). In Mark 11, Jesus became so furious that foreigners couldn't pray in the temple that he drove out the money changers with a whip (we discussed this already in chapter two). Jesus wanted foreigners to pray, to be healed and to be welcomed into relationship with him.

Now let's look at Jesus' familiar parable, often called "The Good Samaritan," a story that illustrates what the Old Testament teaches about caring for foreigners. Jesus has just told the lawyer that his answer—love God with everything (Deut 6:5) and love your neighbor as yourself (Lev 19:18)—deserved an A. The lawyer then asks Jesus, "Who is my *neighbor*?"

> Jesus replied, "A man was going down from Jerusalem to Jericho, and he fell among robbers, who stripped him and beat him and departed, leaving him half dead. Now by chance a priest was going down that road, and when he *saw him* he passed by on the other side. So likewise a Levite, when he came to the place and *saw him*, passed by on the other side. But a Samaritan, as he journeyed, came to where he was, and when he *saw him*, he had compassion. He went to him and bound up his wounds, pouring on oil and wine. Then he set him on his own animal and brought him to an inn and took care of him. And the next day he took out two denarii and gave them to the innkeeper, saying, 'Take care of him, and whatever more you spend, I will repay you when I come back.' Which of these three, do you think, proved to be a neighbor to the man who fell among the robbers?" He said, "The one who showed him

mercy." And Jesus said to him, "You go, and do likewise."
(Lk 10:29-37)

This parable of Jesus is primarily a story about racism. A guy
is robbed, beat up, stripped and left "half dead" (I'm an optimist, so I'd say he was "half alive"). The two guys you'd expect
to help him, the priest and the Levite, *see him* but avoid him.
The next guy shouldn't help him. He's not just a foreigner (we're
assuming the victim is Jewish) but a Samaritan—and Jews
hated Samaritans. (A student told me that in a contemporary
video version he had just seen the "Samaritan" as an Arab taxi
driver.) The Samaritan does a lot of things for the half-dead
guy: heals his wounds, lets him ride his donkey and basically
gives the innkeeper his Visa card. But the most important thing
the Samaritan does—which leads to all his other actions—is
have compassion. Jesus knew that racism could be overcome
only with compassion. The compassion of the Samaritan led
him to acts of extreme hospitality toward someone who probably would have hated him because he was foreign.

Lest we forget, parables are made-up stories. Jesus crafted
this story to shock his listeners about their own racist attitudes
toward Samaritans. The Samaritan, not the priest, was the one
who acted like Elisha as he cared for a foreigner (Naaman). The
Samaritan, not the Levite, was the one who followed the command of Leviticus 19:18 to love his neighbor as himself. While
the lawyer's A answer combined God-love and neighbor-love,
Jesus' story gets an A-plus as it goes beyond simply loving the
neighbor as yourself (Lev 19:18) to include loving the foreigner
as yourself from the same chapter of Leviticus (Lev 19:34), a
verse discussed above. Jesus had to tell this story because the
people of his day were flunking the test of foreigner-love.

If you are from the United States, how would you feel about

a story titled "The Good American"? (If you're Canadian, or
Australian, or whatever, just fill in the blanks accordingly.) As
an American, I would be offended because it suggests that there
is only one good American or at least that good Americans are
rare. It would be hard to interpret the title positively. Doesn't
the title "The Good Samaritan" suggest the same thing about
Samaritans? It sounds racist. It's ironic that Jesus' parable about
not being racist has been given a racist title in our culture. Better titles would be "The Samaritan Neighbor" or "Like a good
neighbor, the Samaritan was there." I think Jesus would have
been offended by our title since he had foreign blood; he told
stories combating racism and he actively loved and welcomed
foreigners.

Talking, Confronting and Befriending

Race continues to be one of the biggest issues facing our world
today. It's hard not to find the topic of race in the pages of a
newspaper or in stories on the evening news. Despite the fact
that both testaments address the topic repeatedly, the Christian
church doesn't seem to be doing any better than the people in
Old-Testament or New-Testament times. There are signs of
hope, as a recent *Time* magazine article discussed how a few
megachurches are helping bridge America's racial divide,[20] but
the article also acknowledged that Sunday morning from
eleven to noon is still the most segregated hour of the week.
So, how can Christians be more like the compassionate, hospitable Samaritan?

First, those of us in the majority culture need to bring up the
topic of race and not simply assume it is an issue only minorities are concerned about. Yahweh and Jesus did not ignore the
issue of race. As we've seen in this chapter, issues surrounding
race and ethnicity come up all over both testaments. Let's dis-

cuss it, preach on it and read about it. But as we discuss the issue of race, let's be sure to spend more time listening than talking.

In the fall of 2009, I taught a class focused on the subject of this book. After discussing the relevant Old Testament texts, I asked the women and minorities in the class to share stories of sexism and racism they had experienced within the context of the church. While I would have hoped that we would be done after only a few minutes, sadly they had plenty of examples, and we ran out of time before everyone could share. For the people who spoke, it was helpful to be listened to, and for the majority culture males, it was a challenging but also enlightening experience.

Second, we confront racism as Jesus did in the Old Testament examples he mentioned in Luke 4 or in the parable he told in Luke 10. Two colleagues of mine recently confronted me about an insensitive racial remark I had made to them. They said that even though they knew I hadn't meant to insult them, they were still deeply offended by my comment. I initially felt very defensive—they should have known that my comments were simply meant to tease them. But then I realized that they had a legitimate point, I didn't understand their context, and my comment had been very hurtful. I asked them questions to understand their perspective and then asked their forgiveness. While their words were hard to hear, I appreciated not only their honesty but also that they valued our relationship enough to confront me.

Third, we make friends with people from other ethnic backgrounds. In the year 1219, while Christians from all over Europe were traveling thousands of miles to kill Muslims, Francis of Assisi traveled thousands of miles to talk to Muslims about Jesus. He famously risked his life in the middle of a siege to befriend one of their leaders, the sultan Malik al-Kamil in Damietta in northeast Egypt, a man as culturally different from Francis as one can imagine. Yet the sultan was impressed by Francis and reportedly said to him, "I would convert to your religion, which is a beautiful one, but I cannot: Both of us would be massacred."[21] If more Christians today practiced hospitality toward people of different races like the Samaritan did in Jesus' parable or befriended people of other faiths (Jewish, Muslim, Buddhist and atheist) like Francis did in Egypt, there would be more Christians.

5

VIOLENT OR PEACEFUL?

A U.S. appeals court recently ruled that the mother of a kindergartner cannot read from the Bible during her son's time of show and tell because of the separation of church and state. In response to the ruling, a letter by Denis of Devon to *The Philadelphia Inquirer* observed that most parents would object to readings in school from *Lady Chatterley's Lover*. Then he asked a provocative question:

> Should it not also be inappropriate for selected readings from a book which glorifies attempted infanticide (Gen 22), gang rape (Judg 19), murder by proxy to satisfy lust for a neighbor's wife (2 Sam 11), and divine mortal retribution for mocking one's elder (2 Kings 2:23)?[1]

Denis of Devon seems to think that because of its content we shouldn't read the Bible to children. While I never read *Lady Chatterley's Lover* to my sons (they would have been bored or grossed out), I read the Bible to them frequently when they were young. The main problem with Denis's letter, however, is his premise that to record something you are somehow glorifying it. By his logic, we shouldn't read the *Philadelphia Inquirer* because it records—and therefore glorifies—murder, warfare, terrorism and rape.

I read the *Inquirer* (and the Bible) daily, and I enjoy trying to determine the perspective of the journalist toward the topic she is writing about. The Holocaust Museum in Washington, D.C., tells the story of what happened to the Jews in World War II, not to glorify in any way the evil actions of the Nazis, but to help its visitors remember the tragedy and to warn against the dangers of racism combined with violence. Similarly, we need to examine the context of a biblical story to determine whether the action is condemned or praised by the text.

Not surprisingly, all of Denis's examples come from the Old Testament; but the text doesn't glorify the violent crimes he lists. Genesis 22 is a difficult passage, but the main point of the story is that Yahweh does not require child sacrifice, unlike the "gods" of Abraham's neighbors. The perspective of the text toward the men who committed the gang rape in Judges is highly negative, and the outrage of the men of Israel against the perpetrators of this heinous crime leads to a civil war (Judg 19–21). David's murder and adultery is not praised but is strongly condemned by Yahweh and his prophet (2 Sam 11:27–12:12). In the next section we will discuss Elisha's violent reaction to being mocked, so I won't go into detail here except to say that his behavior is defensible.

The Bible includes numerous examples of violent behavior, but we shouldn't assume that simply because these stories are included in the Old Testament that the behavior is being condoned. When the God of the Old Testament acts violently, he does it for a reason, and he also frequently acts to promote peace.

Elisha, the Boys and the Bears

Elisha, the boys and the bears. It sounds like a story a parent would tell a young child at bedtime . . . until you actually read it in the Bible.

> He went up from there to Bethel, and while he was going up on the way, some small boys came out of the city and jeered at him, saying, "Go up, you baldhead! Go up, you baldhead!" And he turned around, and when he saw them, he cursed them in the name of the LORD. And two she-bears came out of the woods and tore forty-two of the boys. From there he went on to Mount Carmel, and from there he returned to Samaria. (2 Kings 2:23-25)

Elisha is traveling to Bethel, and along the way he encounters some boys who call him "baldhead." He curses the children in the name of Yahweh. Two bears emerge from the woods. The bears attack the boys, and Elisha continues on his way. For those of us losing our hair, we might think it is totally justified to punish anyone who dares to insult our ever-expanding bald spot (the bears would have finished off my sons a long time ago).

But most readers are justifiably troubled by this story, for three main reasons. First, Elisha was a prophet of God. Shouldn't someone as holy as Elisha have been able to control his anger? Second, the boys seem to be young and innocent. Kids, after all, say the darndest things. Why hold a harmless insult against them? Third, and most significantly, Yahweh seemed to be the primary one behind the attack. The curse was in Yahweh's name, and the bears appear supernaturally. Yahweh must have been the primary cause of the bears' sudden assault. It seems that both Yahweh and his prophet easily become violent, and these young boys paid the price.

Infidel Guy

When I was teaching a class on this topic, I ran across the website of Infidel Guy, an avowed atheist who blogged about this story and asked the question "Would you worship a god that kills children for just calling a man bald?"[2] I made Infidel Guy's blog assigned reading for the class. Based on our classroom discussion, I wrote a reply that we then posted on his website. Here is our response to Infidel Guy:

> We appreciated your passion and insights. We thought you made a great point that this story isn't taught in Sunday school. We think it should be. We also agreed that it is a highly troubling text, and we all felt uncomfortable that it is in the Bible.
>
> However, there are three points that we think you should consider. First, there are two Hebrew words for boys (naar: 2:23 and yeled: 2:24) in the passage.[3] Both words can mean "boy," or even "young boy," but can also mean "adolescent" or "older teenager" (see the Hebrew lexicon of Brown, Driver and Briggs). Both words are even used for Joseph's brother Benjamin when he was in his 20s (Gen 44:20). Since the words have a broad range of meaning, one needs to look at the context to understand how it should be translated. It is unreasonable to assume that a large group of very young boys were hanging out in the wilderness, unsupervised. Nursery schools don't typically meet in the hills outside of town without parents or adult supervision. However, a gang of teenagers could reasonably be by themselves outside of town. Thus, this was not harmless teasing by a group of preschoolers, but serious taunting by a pack of teens. It is reasonable to assume that Elisha's life was in danger. It is

certainly not unthinkable that they were planning to rough him up a bit.

Second, in the United States we say "names will never hurt us" (which really isn't true), but in the rest of the world, and throughout history, insults are taken far more seriously than they are here. We would doubt that your point about a harmless insult would be taken seriously by someone in the Middle East today. They would say what Elisha did was proper. People could be severely punished for insulting leaders, rulers, kings, etc. Think about the whole idea of dueling: you insult my honor, and we will battle to the death. While in our 21st-century, Western mindset it may seem like Elisha was overreacting, within his cultural context his behavior was justified.

Third, as one studies the broader context of 2 Kings (chapters 2-6, 8, 13), in Elisha one sees an individual who heals the sick (including Naaman, a foreign general), feeds the hungry, purifies poisoned water, prays for a barren woman who then gives birth, raises the dead and prevents a war. Even the touching of his bones resurrects a corpse (2 Kings 13:21). So, his life was characterized by miraculous acts of service, worthy of Mother Teresa or Jesus. Apparently all of these deeds of Elisha are performed with divine blessing. God must have helped him do these good works. You may be the sort of person who devotes large amounts of your time caring for the sick, the homeless and the widows just like Elisha did, but we know that we don't spend nearly as much time and energy caring for people as he did. The merciful behavior that he practiced everywhere else in 2 Kings leads us to conclude that we shouldn't view his actions with the bears in isolation. Even though the

story of the bears is troubling to us, we will give Elisha
the benefit of the doubt given all of his other amazing
acts of compassion.[4]

Violence to Save Life

We received no reply to our post. I imagine someone could respond that Yahweh overreacted to any possible threat here. Infidel Guy assumes that the forty-two boys were killed by the bears. The text, however, doesn't suggest death was the result; it simply states they were "mauled" or "torn." If these youths were killed, the text would make that clear. Just a few chapters earlier (1 Kings 13:24; 20:36), two separate incidents are recorded of lion attacks, and in both instances the text makes it explicit that the victim was not just mauled or torn but was actually killed by the animal. The attack here by the bears on these teenagers was violent but not fatal.

The main point of the story, however, is not that Yahweh picks on children but rather that Yahweh protected the life of Elisha. To add support to the idea that Elisha's life was in danger from this gang of over forty teenagers, a series of manuscripts of the Septuagint (the Greek version of the Old Testament) records that the boys also threw stones at Elisha, which could easily have killed an old man. A cynic might say the Septuagint just added the details about the stoning of Elisha to justify his violent reaction, but it is more reasonable to assume that Elisha had a strong reason to be worried about his own life—they really were trying to stone him. Otherwise, why would he send bears to attack these teenagers immediately after he had just saved the lives of many people from their own city by purifying their poisoned water source (2 Kings 2:19-22)? Elisha didn't start the fight but was simply acting in self-defense.

Why would Yahweh want to make the point so dramatically that he would protect the life of his prophet? To answer this question, we need to think about what it was like to be a prophet. Prophets during the time of Elisha led a tough life. It would have been difficult for prophets to get a life insurance policy. They were frequently mocked, despised, persecuted, tortured and killed (1 Kings 18:4, 14; 2 Chron 36:15-16; Jer 20:2; 38:1-6; Ezek 2:6; Mt 5:12; 23:30-37; Heb 11:32-38).

We don't know why Elisha is protected here by God, while in other situations God allows prophets to suffer, but to focus on one instance where Yahweh protects a prophet seems to miss the big picture of what the life of prophet involved. The fact that Yahweh rescued Elisha meant not only that Yahweh wanted to send a message that Elisha would have divine protection, but also that he wanted Elisha to continue in his ministry of compassion. I don't fully understand the severity of God's violent reaction here, but I am glad that Yahweh protected Elisha from a teenage gang so the prophet could go on to bless the lives of thousands of others.

Yahweh protected Elisha so he could bless the sick and the hungry and widows and orphans. Would it have been good for the assassination attempt of Claus von Stauffenberg (the character played by Tom Cruise in the 2008 film *Valkyrie*) against Adolf Hitler to succeed? I think so. If the assassination and subsequent coup had been successful and World War II had ended almost a year earlier, perhaps hundreds of thousands of lives could have been saved. Similarly, I believe that Yahweh's violent intervention on behalf of Elisha against this teenage gang saved lives. Not all violent incidents in the Old Testament are resolved so easily, but a pattern emerges that Yahweh is willing to punish individuals and even nations severely to protect the weak and preserve life.

The Canaanites (Again)

We've discussed the Canaanites in the context of anger (chapter two) and racism (chapter four), but since the conquest narrative also involves divine violence, it is necessary to review the subject here. Previously we noted five things about the violence involved with the conquest narratives. First, the Canaanites were being punished for their wicked and violent behavior, particularly attacking defenseless Israel as they were fleeing a situation in which they had been oppressively enslaved for hundreds of years. Second, Israel was not trying to brutally expand their borders to establish an empire like the Assyrians, but as exiles they were simply attempting to reestablish a home in the land of their ancestors. Third, Yahweh had been slow to punish the Canaanites, waiting during the entire period of Israelite enslavement (Gen 15:16), giving the Canaanites plenty of time to repent. Fourth, the Canaanite conquest was not unusual, because in the ancient Near East, military victors *typically* either killed or enslaved all the vanquished people. Fifth, the killing was probably limited and localized as only a few texts speak of widespread destruction, while most of them speak of numerous Canaanites remaining in the land.

One additional point to make here is that the primary image used to describe the Canaanite conquest is not of slaughter. While the texts that describe Israel's violent obedience get our attention (Josh 10:40; 11:12), the textual image used far more frequently for the conquest is "driving out" the people of the land (Ex 23:28-31; 34:11; Num 32:21; 33:52-55; Deut 4:38; 7:1; 9:3-6; 11:23; 18:12; 33:27; Josh 3:10; 14:12; 17:18; 23:5). Yahweh tells the Israelites that he will drive out the people of the land before the Israelites even arrive, using hornets and angels (Ex 23:28; 33:2). The number of Canaanites in the land appears to have been reduced before the conquest battles begin. The books of Joshua and Judges also repeatedly tell us not only that Israel didn't slaughter all the Canaanites, but they didn't even successfully drive them out (Josh 13:13; 15:63; 16:10; 17:13; 23:13; Judg 1:19, 21, 27-33; 2:21).

Although these texts clearly view Israel's unsuccessful attempts to clear out the land negatively, Yahweh's voice is noticeably absent from these sections of Joshua and Judges. The problem for Yahweh wasn't that his people were not violent enough toward the Canaanites, but that since the Canaanites weren't completely driven out, Israel fell into idolatry (Judg 2:11-23).

While we might think that "driving out a people" still sounds brutally violent, Yahweh's goal back in Egypt was to make Pharaoh "drive out" the Israelites (Ex 6:1; 11:1). If Yahweh wanted his own people to be driven out by Pharaoh, we don't need to assume it was a violent process. Israel underwent a divinely initiated, forced migration, as did many of the Canaanite people. The Canaanite conquest was violent but not unusual, harsh, cruel or unjustified.

Disturbing Divine Behavior?

At this point I need to mention a 2009 book by Old Testament scholar Eric Seibert, titled *Disturbing Divine Behavior: Troubling Old Testament Images of God*. Seibert focuses particularly on troubling images of divine violence, such as the Canaanite slaughter. His book has much to commend. It is well written and well researched, and he is willing to examine problematic texts (many of which I discuss in chapters two, four and five). He raises great questions about how we understand these passages.

But I can't agree with his central thesis. Seibert reconciles the loving God of the New Testament and the harsh God of the Old Testament by saying, basically, that the harsh God of the Old Testament doesn't exist. He argues that Old Testament passages that describe a violent God can be rejected because that behavior is inconsistent with the character of God revealed by Jesus in the Gospels. So, if a text portrays Yahweh as acting violently, it didn't actually happen. Seibert would, therefore, end up rejecting major sections of the Old Testament, a bit like Marcion.

While I find his conclusion attractive in one sense (the problem does disappear), I am unwilling to reject large sections of the Old Testament because the God it portrays doesn't fit my perception of what he should be like. I continue to be troubled by Old Testament images of God, but I will work to understand them better by continuing to study the text on its own, within its biblical context and within its ancient Near Eastern context.

185,000 Bodies

Perhaps the most dramatic example of divine violence in the Old Testament is the following report of a slaughter of the Assyrians, who were besieging the city of Jerusalem, by an angel of Yahweh during the reign of Hezekiah:

> And that night the angel of the LORD went out and struck down 185,000 in the camp of the Assyrians. And when people arose early in the morning, behold, these were all dead bodies. (2 Kings 19:35)

One hundred eighty-five thousand bodies. No other divine act of violence in the Old Testament has casualties of this magnitude. The size of the slaughter is shocking. Many commentators think that the numbers here are hyperbolic,[5] but even if we are to conclude a textual exaggeration is involved, it doesn't remove the problem of a divinely initiated slaughter of massive proportion. Why did God kill so many people? I see three reasons.

First, people get killed in contexts of war. The men killed were all soldiers who were attempting to capture Jerusalem. Only about twenty years earlier (722 B.C.), Assyria had destroyed Israel and its capital, Samaria. At this point (701 B.C.), Sennacherib's army was attempting to destroy Judah and its capital, Jerusalem. On this campaign the Assyrians had already captured numerous other fortified Judean cities (2 Kings 18:13). These men had already killed many Judeans. Yahweh was fighting defensively to protect Judah from an Assyrian invasion.

Second, Assyria was a brutally violent nation. I mentioned in chapter four how Ashurnasirpal of Assyria bragged about burning, mutilating and hanging captives, including boys and girls. Here Sennacherib's ambassador had already prophesied to the people of Jerusalem that they were doomed to "eat their own dung and drink their own urine" (2 Kings 18:27 NRSV). The city of Nineveh was the capital of Assyria, and the book of Jonah describes how their wickedness warranted divine condemnation (Jon 1:1; 3:10). Many Assyrians were killed, but they were not the victims of the story. Assyria was the aggressor nation attempting to conquer, seize tribute and expand its empire.

Third, the Assyrians mocked Yahweh, declaring that he couldn't deliver Israel from the power of Sennacherib, their emperor (2 Kings 18:32-35; 19:4, 10, 22-23). While Sennacherib thought Yahweh wasn't powerful enough to defeat him, Yahweh didn't agree. Sennacherib must not have known the first rule of trash-talking. If you are going to talk trash, you need to back it up. When Yahweh talked smack against Sennacherib (2 Kings 19:28), he followed through in dramatic fashion, destroying Sennacherib's army and delivering the people of Judah. Yahweh's violence was justified in this context of war against a brutal empire to defend his honor.

Simple, Swift and Straightforward

Yahweh was willing to use violence in specific instances to protect Elisha and Jerusalem, and as we examine laws concerning violence in Exodus, Leviticus and Deuteronomy, we can determine his attitude toward violent behavior more generally. We learn a lot about Yahweh's values by looking at how he legislated for his people to live peacefully.[6]

It is first necessary to point out that Israel's justice system was very different from our own. We can't naively assume that their system was similar to our overly complicated matrix of jails, prisons, lawyers, trials, appeals and levels of local, state, district and national courts. In ancient Israel, a city was lucky to have a judge (Deut 16:18-20). Justice, therefore, needed to be simple, swift and straightforward. While we might throw a criminal into prison to serve time, that wasn't an option in Israel, particularly during their wilderness wanderings when their laws were given. A violent sentence was usually the only option to punish a violent crime.

Even with this acknowledgment, Israel's laws can still seem draconian. While most modern readers wouldn't be shocked to learn that murder was a capital offense in Israel (Ex 21:14), one might be surprised to learn that rape and kidnapping were also punishable by death (Deut 22:25; 24:7). Though these penalties seem harsh, in the context of ancient Israel they were necessary for two reasons. First, rapists and kidnappers typically targeted weaker members of society, so the death penalty would serve as a major disincentive to reduce these violent crimes and protect women who might have been raped and the poor who might have been kidnapped to be sold as slaves. Yahweh's extreme concern for the poor can also be seen in his declaration that he would "kill with the sword" people who oppress widows and orphans (Ex 22:22-24). Yahweh wanted his people to know that he would violently protect the powerless of society.

Second, the alternative punishment, a fine that was prescribed in ancient Near Eastern law codes, would serve merely as a "slap on the wrist" for wealthy members of society who could easily pay it. Therefore, these severe punishments mandated by Yahweh would not only reduce violent crime, they would also foster a more just society.

An Eye for an Eye, a Wedgie for a Wedgie

Another law that seems unnecessarily harsh is the "eye for an eye" law, also called *lex talionis*, or law of exact equivalence. Many people are familiar with Jesus' radical response to this law in the Sermon on the Mount, in which he tells his listeners to "turn the other cheek" (Mt 5:39). But the clearest expression of this law appears in Leviticus.

> If anyone injures his neighbor, as he has done it shall be done to him, fracture for fracture, eye for eye, tooth for tooth; whatever injury he has given a person shall be given to him. (Lev 24:19-20)

If you injure another person's bone, eye or tooth, as punishment your bone, eye or tooth will be injured similarly. Christians today are called by Jesus not to respond with an eye for an eye, but with turning the other cheek, going the second mile and loving our enemies (Mt 5:38-44). (Recently, one of my sons gave the other a wedgie. While chasing the perpetrator, the victim yelled out, "An eye for an eye, a wedgie for a wedgie." While fleeing, the perpetrator replied, "You're supposed to turn the other cheek.")

Just as Jesus' commands from the Sermon on the Mount were progressive for first-century Israel, the *lex talionis* principle was progressive for ancient Israel. Old Testament scholar David Baker describes the societal benefits of *lex talionis*: "It limits vengeance and rules out punishment disproportionate to the offense."[7] As anyone with sons knows, the pattern that usually follows violence is not equivalent retaliation but escalation. You pinch me, I hit your arm. You hit my arm, I punch your face. On a national scale the escalation principle, if left unchecked, eventually results in war. An eye for an eye, therefore, limits the violence, resulting in simple, swift and straightforward justice in a world without an overly complicated legal system.

While Yahweh's legal punishments seem violent, they were actually effective means of reducing violent crime and promoting peace among his people. Personally, I'm glad that the God of the Old Testament took extreme measures to care for the poor and the powerless and to prevent bloodshed and war.

Elisha, the Kings and the Horses

Elisha, the kings and the horses. Unlike the story we looked at in the beginning of the chapter, this one can be told to young children. In that story, Yahweh acted violently to protect Elisha from harm. In this story, Yahweh and Elisha promote peace between Israel and Syria, two nations that had been at war for literally hundreds of years. Elisha (also called "the man of God" here) kept warning the king of Israel about the Syrian king's troop movements, so the Syrian king decided to capture Elisha inside his own city.

> So he sent there horses and chariots and a great army, and they came by night and surrounded the city.
> When the servant of the man of God rose early in the

morning and went out, behold, an army with horses and chariots was all around the city. And the servant said, "Alas, my master! What shall we do?" He said, "Do not be afraid, for those who are with us are more than those who are with them." Then Elisha **prayed** and said, "O LORD, please open his eyes that he may see." So the LORD opened the eyes of the young man, and he saw, and behold, the mountain was full of horses and chariots of fire all around Elisha. And when the Syrians came down against him, Elisha **prayed** to the LORD and said, "Please strike this people with blindness." So he struck them with blindness in accordance with the prayer of Elisha. And Elisha said to them, "This is not the way, and this is not the city. Follow me, and I will bring you to the man whom you seek." And he led them to Samaria. As soon as they entered Samaria, Elisha said, "O LORD, open the eyes of these men, that they may see." So the LORD opened their eyes and they saw, and behold, they were in the midst of Samaria.

As soon as the king of Israel saw them, he said to Elisha, "My father, shall I strike them down? Shall I strike them down?" He answered, "You shall not strike them down. Would you strike down those whom you have taken captive with your sword and with your bow? Set bread and water before them, that they may eat and drink and go to their master." So he prepared for them a great feast, and when they had eaten and drunk, he sent them away, and they went to their master. And the Syrians did not come again on raids into the land of Israel. (2 Kings 6:14-23)

The first thing to note here is that, once again, Elisha's life was in danger. He and his servant were surrounded by an army with horses and chariots, and the situation was sufficiently threatening to cause the servant to panic. Elisha, however, was confident that he and the servant were safe, because he knew that God had protected him in the past, particularly when he was in danger from the teenage gang. Instead of bears, this time Yahweh sent horses and chariots in a vision of fire.[8]

While it may appear that Yahweh didn't play a significant role in this cessation of hostilities, Elisha knew better. In the beginning, middle and end of the crisis, Elisha *prayed* (2 Kings 6:17, 18, 20). In response to these prayers, Yahweh opened the eyes of the servant to see the vision, he closed the eyes of the Syrians so they could be led into Samaria, and he opened the eyes of the Syrians inside Samaria.

Ironically, even in the midst of Yahweh's effort here to promote peace, he did some serious smiting. He "smote" the Syrians with blindness. Wherever the English Standard Version uses a form of "strike," the King James Version uses a form of "smite." Despite being "smitten," none of the Syrians are permanently hurt, because their sight is soon restored. The king of Israel, however, wants to really "smite" them, permanently. But Elisha says no. Not only does he refuse to allow the Syrians to be slaughtered, he commands that they be fed. (Elisha must have read chapter four about showing hospitality to foreigners.) The king of Israel then prepares a feast for his enemies, and Syria and Israel are at peace.[9] So this time Yahweh's "smiting" doesn't result in violence but peace. Yahweh and Elisha deserve a joint Nobel Peace Prize for their active role in bringing two enemy nations to a truce.

While Jesus tends to get exclusive credit for the "love your enemies" idea (Mt 5:44), the inspiration for it comes from the God of the Old Testament, from stories like Elisha, the kings and the horses. There are many other examples of peacemaking in the Old Testament. Elisha's Syrian strategy seems to come straight out of the book of Proverbs: "If your enemy is hungry, give him bread to eat, / and if he is thirsty, give him water to drink" (Prov 25:21). As we saw in chapter four, Elisha and the slave girl both loved their enemy, the Syrian general Naaman, who was healed from leprosy. David could have easily killed his enemy Saul on two occasions but refused because he knew Yahweh would not have approved (1 Sam 24:3-7; 26:7-12). The three wise women of Samuel mentioned in chapter three (Abigail, the woman of Tekoa, the woman of Abel) acted as divine peacemakers and used their wisdom to prevent bloodshed (1 Sam 25; 2 Sam 14; 20). While Jonah didn't want to love his Assyrian enemies, Yahweh gave him no choice, and the Ninevites eventually repented (Jon 3). In Jeremiah's letter, Yahweh told the exiles in Babylon to love their enemies: "Seek the welfare of the city where I have sent you into exile, and pray to the LORD on its behalf, for in its welfare you will find your welfare" (Jer 29:7). In a prophetic vision of the future found in both Isaiah and Micah, after Yahweh teaches everyone his ways, swords become unnecessary and are beaten into plowshares, and nations stop fighting each other (Is 2:4; Mic 4:3). Because the God of the Old Testament is a God of peace, he wanted his people to be at peace with their neighbors.

Sword-Wielding Jesus or Peace-Bringing Jesus?

We are familiar with Jesus' teaching in the Sermon on the Mount to turn the other cheek, to love enemies and to pray for your persecutors (Mt 5:39, 44). Because of these teachings, even atheists like Richard Dawkins like Jesus. Famous nonviolent heroes of the twentieth century such as Martin Luther King Jr. and Mahatma Gandhi looked to Jesus for inspiration for their ideals.

But Jesus also told his disciples that he came not to bring

peace but a sword (Mt 10:34; Lk 12:51). A sword-wielding Jesus? That sounds like what the God of the Old Testament is supposed to be like. However, by speaking of bringing a sword, Jesus wasn't going against his own advice in the Sermon on the Mount, but was simply warning his followers that their choice to follow him would cause major tension, particularly among family members.

Jesus was rarely in sword-wielding mode and was often in peacemaking mode. He frequently brought peace into troubled situations. After forgiving the sins of a woman who was probably a prostitute, he told her, "Go in peace," and after healing a woman who had a twelve-year blood hemorrhage, he told her, "Go in peace" (Lk 7:50; 8:48). When Jesus first appeared to his fearful disciples after his resurrection, he delivered a similar message of peace.

> On the evening of that day, the first day of the week, the doors being locked where the disciples were for fear of the Jews, Jesus came and stood among them and said to them, "*Peace be with you.*" When he had said this, he showed them his hands and his side. Then the disciples were glad when they saw the Lord. Jesus said to them again, "*Peace be with you.* As the Father has sent me, even so I am sending you." And when he had said this, he breathed on them and said to them, "Receive the Holy Spirit. If you forgive the sins of any, they are forgiven them; if you withhold forgiveness from any, it is withheld."
>
> Now Thomas, one of the Twelve, called the Twin, was not with them when Jesus came. So the other disciples told him, "We have seen the Lord." But he said to them, "Unless I see in his hands the mark of the nails, and place

my finger into the mark of the nails, and place my hand into his side, I will never believe."

Eight days later, his disciples were inside again, and Thomas was with them. Although the doors were locked, Jesus came and stood among them and said, *"Peace be with you."* (Jn 20:19-26)

The disciples' fear here was understandable, since their Lord had just been killed and they would have been next on the hit list. Jesus' first post-resurrection words were also some of his final words to his disciples. He knew that at this critical time in their mentoring, the disciples didn't need a sword-wielder but a peace-bringer, so he blessed them three times with the words *"Peace be with you."*

We should also remember that Jesus gave two gifts here to empower his disciples and eventually the early church: the gifts of peace and of the Holy Spirit. Interestingly, the church in Judea, Galilee and Samaria is characterized in the book of Acts as having peace and walking in the Spirit (Acts 9:31).

Since we typically undervalue the impact of spoken words, it seems weird for peace to be given as a gift when Jesus talked. But Jesus knew the power of speaking a blessing of peace to his disciples. He knew that his words "Peace be with you" had power to remove their fear. In the book of Acts, the disciples are characterized by boldness in the face of death (Acts 4:13, 29, 31; 28:31). The peace of Jesus was powerful. The gift of peace had such a profound impact on Paul that he passed on the blessing of peace in the introduction of every one of his letters (Rom 1:7; 1 Cor 1:3; 2 Cor 1:2; and so on).

After passing the peace to his disciples, Jesus showed them the wounds on his hands and on his side. He knew that the holes in his own body were proof of his love for his enemies. To use language from Paul, while we were his enemies, Jesus' death reconciled us to God (Rom 5:8-10). Because of Jesus' willingness to be a voluntary victim of violence, we were reconciled with God. It was the ultimate act of peacemaking.

Jesus' peacemaking behavior at the end of John's Gospel reminds us of what we've seen so far about the God of the Old Testament, but I'll briefly mention two other Old Testament connections. First, Yahweh's Messiah was prophesied to be a Prince of Peace (Is 9:6), which fits Jesus perfectly. Second, the God of the Old Testament also delivered a peaceful message identical to that of Jesus. Over a thousand years before Christ, when Gideon was cowering in fear, Yahweh told him, *"Peace be with you,"* and Gideon responded by building an altar and declaring, "Yahweh is peace!" (Judg 6:23-24).

Promote Peace and Reconciliation

Yahweh and Jesus both bring peace into situations of crisis, trouble and fear, but they also both wield the sword. How then do we decide when to be sword-wielders and when to be peacemakers? We start by acknowledging that both Yahweh and Jesus prefer peace to violence. Yahweh used violence only to punish the wicked or to protect the weak, and he ultimately promoted peace within Israel and between Israel and her neighbors. Jesus in only one context said he didn't bring peace; everywhere else he blessed people with peace, he promoted reconciliation, and he was willing to be victimized by violence to restore peace. We should, therefore, prefer peace to violence.

How then can we promote peace like Yahweh and Jesus? Elisha healed and fed his enemies, and Jesus told us to love and pray for our enemies. So, promote peace by healing, feeding, loving and praying for enemies. But you may say, "Who's my enemy?" Most of us don't think we have enemies, except perhaps while we're driving or when we're talking politics. Jesus said that thinking violent thoughts about a person or even calling someone a fool is equivalent to murder (Mt 5:21-26). By Jesus' definition, there are many undocumented homicides on the roads and in political discussions. We all should spend more time praying for our "enemies" while driving and discussing.

In the fall of 2001 we were living in student housing at Oxford, England, surrounded by people from all over the world, including a Muslim family from Libya. Since the United States and Libya did not have good diplomatic relations, we had never met a Libyan before. Shortly after 9/11, my wife, Shannon, was praying, and she felt like God was telling her to invite the Libyan family over for dinner. She personally didn't think it would be a good idea. It could be awkward. *Hey, your country and my country hate each other. Muslim terrorists just killed thousands of Americans in New York and D.C. Let's talk.*

But God kept bringing our Libyan neighbors to mind, so eventually Shannon went down and knocked on their door. The father answered. Shannon paused. Awkward silence. Eventually she said, "We know you're Muslim. You know we're Christians. But we'd like to invite you over for dinner." More awkward silence.

Then he teared up and said, "No Christian has ever invited us to dinner. We would be delighted to join you." We had a great time together over dinner, first at our flat, then later at their flat. That December, Shannon organized a nativity play for our housing complex. Participants included Christian children from the United States and Australia, Jewish boys from Israel (the shepherds) and Muslim children from Libya (the wise men). In his incarnation, Jesus came to bring peace on earth and to reconcile people to each other and to God.

6

LEGALISTIC OR GRACIOUS?

Does Calvin (the comic strip character, not the theologian) sound like any deity you know?

> *Calvin to himself:* First there was nothing and then there was Calvin! Calvin, the mighty God, creates the universe with pure will! From utter nothingness comes swirling form! Life begins where once was void! But Calvin is no kind and loving god. He's one of the old gods! He demands sacrifice! Yes, Calvin is a god of the underworld! And the puny inhabitants of the earth despise him! The great Calvin ignores their pleas for mercy and the doomed writhe in agony!
>
> *Calvin's father to Calvin's mother:* Have you seen how absorbed Calvin is with those Tinker Toys? He's creating whole worlds in there!
>
> *Calvin's mother to Calvin's father:* I bet he grows up to be an architect.[1]

The god-Calvin manifests many of the popular perceptions of Yahweh: an all-powerful creator of the universe, not a kind or loving god, an old (Testament?) god and a sacrifice-demanding god. Calvin sounds more like the God of the Old Testament than the New Testament. Jesus says he "desires mercy not sacrifice" (Lk 2:24), but Yahweh goes on for chapters describing in detail the sacrifices he "demands" (Lev 1–7).[2] Apparently, even Calvin perceives the God of the Old Testament negatively (surely Hobbes has a more favorable impression).

Calvin isn't the only one who perceives the Old Testament God and his laws negatively. For an assignment in one of my classes, students needed to survey attitudes about God. To the question "How has God been presented to you?" one respondent replied, "Someone who does not like me unless I follow his boring rules." Apparently God's rules are boring and are used by God to determine whether or not he likes people.

In an episode of *The Simpsons*, Lisa needs to rescue her baby sister, Maggie, from a convent while the nuns are singing, "If you're happy and you know it, it's a sin."[3] If sinning makes you happy, then keeping God's laws is going to be really depressing. God's laws don't seem very appealing, as if he designed them to ruin our enjoyment.

With laws that are demanding, boring and no fun, God could appear to be legalistic. Legalists are obsessed with the law and have lost sight of its purpose. They have no room for grace in their interpretation of law. Legalists will, therefore, make laws that are demanding, strict, boring, arbitrary and oppressive. So, is the God of the Old Testament legalistic, as he is perceived in *Calvin and Hobbes*, in my student's survey response and in *The Simpsons*? (Oh, but just to set the record straight, Jesus' quote that he desires mercy not sacrifice actually comes originally from the Old Testament, from Hosea 6:6.) As we examine various laws of the Old Testament, we'll discover that Yahweh is far from being legalistic. Let's begin with a question.

Have a Lot of Sex and Eat a Lot of Food

What's the first command in the Bible? It's not "Don't eat the apple from that tree." In fact, it isn't a prohibition at all but a positive command to do something enjoyable.

> And God *blessed* them. And **God** said to them, "Be fruitful and multiply and fill the earth." (Gen 1:28)

God first commands the humans to "be fruitful and multiply." This is not only the first command in the Bible; it is actually the very first words God speaks to the humans, so we know it is important. I'm no expert on the subject, but if God's image-bearers are going to follow the divine directive to be fruitful, then sex is probably going to be necessary. In fact, they aren't just supposed to multiply; they are commanded to "fill the earth." That sounds like a lot of sex. So, God's first command is basically, "Have a lot of sex." God's laws don't seem too bad so far.

What's the second command in the Bible? This one is actually about eating, but perhaps not what you think.

> And the LORD **God** commanded the man, saying, "You may *surely* eat of *every* tree of the garden, but of the tree of the knowledge of good and evil you shall not eat, for in the day that you eat of it you shall surely die." (Gen 2:16-17)

Yahweh commands the man, "Eat!" or more literally, "Eat, eat!" In the Hebrew, an infinitive form of the verb eat (*akal*) is repeated for adverbial emphasis, rendered well by New Revised Standard Version as "freely eat."[4] Yahweh even told the man to freely eat from every tree in the garden. And there were a lot of trees to choose from because Yahweh had "stocked the fridge" by filling the garden of Eden with a wide variety of fruit trees that looked good and tasted good (Gen 2:9).

God's second command isn't just "eat," but "eat a lot of food." While some people might say the actual command doesn't come until Genesis 2:17 in the prohibition to eat from the tree of the knowledge of good and evil, the Hebrew would suggest otherwise. The verbs in both verse 16 and verse 17 are the same form (imperfects), which can have an imperative force. So God commanded, "Eat, eat!" before he commanded, "Don't eat!"

I realize people may have a problem with how I'm expressing these first two commands, since we live in a world already obsessed with sex and food. I do not want to appear overly hedonistic or insensitive to people without spouses or to people with eating disorders or weight problems. But Christians are often justifiably perceived in popular culture as being uptight and legalistic (particularly in the realm of sex), which can ironically contribute to the cultural obsession problem. So it is good to be reminded that God's first two commands shockingly affirm the goodness of his creation and his desire that we delight in his gifts of sexuality and food.

Why does God initiate his relationship with his subjects by commanding them to have a lot of sex and eat a lot of food? Because he is generous and not legalistic. Sex and food were two great gifts God gave the humans. So he commanded the humans to enjoy them. He clearly wanted the humans to be happy. As we look at other passages, we'll see that God's generosity, goodness and graciousness are the foundation for all his laws.

Notice that right before the command in Genesis 1:28 to multiply, the text tells us that God *blessed* them. The English Standard Version separates the blessing from the first command with a period, making them two distinct actions, but the New International Version links them into one action: "God blessed them and said to them," which not only receives support from the Hebrew but also makes more sense. The actualization of God's multiplication commission (sex) was designed to be a blessing.

The Old Testament begins by revealing a highly generous God who wants to bless the humans he created. These first two commands tell us a lot about the character of God. While the rest of God's laws may not be as obviously enjoyable as the commands to breed and feast, we need to remember how the relationship between God and his people began as we examine other Old Testament legal texts. We should read other Old Testament commands through the lens of a God who wants to bless and be generous.

Could It Be . . . Satan?

How did the amazingly generous God of the Old Testament somehow get the image of being a legalistic spoilsport? Could it be . . . Satan? Actually, yes, that's exactly what Satan does. We already discussed Genesis 3 in chapter three, but we ignored the role of the serpent there, so we'll look at it here. While Genesis 3 doesn't equate the serpent and Satan, in his primary role as tempter, the serpent here is at least serving the purposes of Satan.[5]

> Now the serpent was more crafty than any other beast of the field that the LORD God had made.
>
> He said to the woman, "Did God *actually* say, 'You shall **not** eat of *any* tree in the garden'?" And the woman said to the serpent, "We may eat of the fruit of the trees in the garden, but God said, 'You shall not eat of the fruit of the tree that is in the midst of the garden, neither shall you touch it, lest you die.'" But the serpent said to the woman, "You will not surely die. For God knows that when you eat

of it your eyes will be opened, and you will be like God, knowing good and evil." (Gen 3:1-5)

The serpent's first words to the woman, "Did God *actually* say, 'You shall *not* eat of *any* tree in the garden'?" could be loosely paraphrased, "I know God is mean, stingy and legalistic, but is he *really* that mean, stingy and legalistic that he won't let you eat *anything*?" Mean because he doesn't want them to eat any of the wonderful fruit. Stingy because he doesn't want to share with them. Legalistic because he wants to command them and deprive them of good things. Notice that the serpent doesn't make his point with a statement, but he uses a question that implies it. He's crafty, that serpent.

Look at how the woman responds to the serpent's question. She doesn't say Yahweh told them they could "*freely* eat from *every* tree except one," but merely, "We may eat from the fruit trees in the garden." The generosity of Yahweh takes a serious hit in her response. While Yahweh merely told the humans not to eat the fruit from the one tree, otherwise they would die, she adds that they can't even touch it. Her words make God seem legalistic.

To complicate the issue, Yahweh appears to be wrong and the serpent right, since the two humans don't literally die on the day they eat the fruit. The serpent's negative portrayal of Yahweh has effectively convinced the humans that God's commands are not good for them and that God does not have their best interests in mind.

Even though the serpent, the woman and the man perceive God negatively and his command legalistically, that does not change what God has already done for the humans. So far God has blessed the humans, has commanded them to have a lot of sex and eat a lot of delicious food and has warned them not to eat from only one of the many fruit trees so that they don't die. Despite the words of the serpent, God's deeds revealed his goodness. God's actions define his character, not popular perceptions of his actions.

Genesis begins with the blessing of the first commands, then shifts to the drama of the first temptation, which is followed by the disaster of the first sin. Two crucial lessons can be discerned from this tragic story. First, temptation questions the goodness of God's commands. Second, sin results from perceiving God not as good, generous and gracious, but as mean, stingy and legalistic. A proper understanding of God and his laws is, therefore, vital to resist temptation and avoid sin.

As we think about what survived and what died in Genesis 3, we see further evidence for God's goodness. God's graciousness and not his deceptiveness was the reason he didn't kill the humans instantly after they ate the fruit. God's generosity was the reason he did kill animals to make skins to clothe the two naked and embarrassed humans. There is no evidence so far in the Bible that God is anything other than generous, gracious and good.

Why Do Good Things Happen to Bad People?

People often ask, "Why do bad things happen to good people?"[6] Most people think of themselves as good, so they assume that in a just world they deserve good things and are troubled when bad comes their way. But Scripture informs us that from God's perspective no one is good (Ps 14:3; Rom 3:23). Only once in recorded history did bad things happen to a totally good person—when Jesus died on a cross to reconcile his followers to God.[7] Since I'm bad, in a just world I can expect bad things and should be surprised when I receive good things. So, I ask the question, "Why do good things happen to bad people?"

Good things happen to bad people because God is good. Jesus himself said God is the only one who is good (Mk 10:18). (Jesus was both good and God.) The goodness of Yahweh is a constant refrain in Old Testament worship texts, and Israel repeatedly gave thanks to Yahweh for his goodness. Four psalms begin by thanking God for his goodness (Ps 106; 107; 118; 136). Another psalm uses language from Genesis 2 of God's generous provision of good things for the humans by commanding worshipers to "taste and see that Yahweh is good" (Ps 34:8). Other texts simply state Yahweh is good, usually in contexts of worshiping him for his goodness (1 Chron 16:34; 2 Chron 5:13; 7:3; Ps 100:5; 135:3; 145:9; Jer 33:11; Lam 3:25; Nahum 1:7). In Yahweh's blessing on his people Israel in Ezekiel, he reiterated themes from Genesis 1–2, telling them he will do more good to them than he's ever done before; he will multiply their population and make them fruitful, so that they know he is Yahweh (Ezek 36:9-11). Goodness is such an integral part of Yahweh's character that he cannot help himself; he has to do good. He is the quintessential do-gooder, in the best possible sense.

We, therefore, need to remember that God's goodness is behind all his commands. His commands are meant to bless humans (see Deut 30:11-20). While we have all experienced bad laws or unnecessary laws, if the lawgiver is generous and gracious, his laws will be good.

Many Laws, Random Laws and Harsh Laws

A person might conclude that Yahweh is legalistic because the Old Testament includes many laws, random laws and harsh laws, so let's examine each of those concerns. The Old Testament has a lot of laws, particularly in the Pentateuch: the Covenant Code (Ex 20–23), the Holiness Code (Lev 17–26), the Priestly Code (Ex 25–31; 35–40; Lev 1–16; Num 1–10; 15;

18–20; 26–30; 34–36) and the Deuteronomic Code (Deut 12–26). That's a lot of laws. Why are so many laws necessary?

While we might feel burdened by the tax code every April 15 or by the "Rules of the Road" when we study for our driver's license, in general, laws are good. I hate to pay taxes, but I'm thankful for the things it buys: streets, bridges, schools, welfare and Social Security. When I'm driving down Cowpath Road (my street) and go through a green light, I'm thankful for the law that commands drivers on Bergey Road to stop at a red light. (Although, in my neighborhood, they have to post signs at lights reminding people to "Wait for green." Isn't that what red means?) We don't like to be restricted by laws, but we are glad other people are. Laws are good.

The development of legal codes was definitely a good thing in ancient society. Before law codes, the word of the ruler was law, and his (rarely her) dictates were often corrupt and based on what would give him the most power. The law codes of Ur-Nammu of Ur (2100 B.C.) and Hammurabi of Babylon (1790 B.C.), which predated the Mosaic laws, contributed to economic and political stability in their ancient contexts.

While you might find reading through hundreds of verses of legal material in Leviticus and Numbers tedious, Old Testament law codes are actually concise compared to modern law codes. We've all seen images of a lawyer's office: four walls, each wall lined with ten shelves, each shelf containing a hundred books, each book with thousands of laws, cases and precedents. Yahweh's laws don't even fill up one book. Granted, the Bible is a long book, but far more of its chapters tell stories than record laws.

The reason the Old Testament included laws is that Israel needed a legal system as they transitioned from being an enslaved people to being a nation ruled first by judges and then by kings. The Old Testament legal corpus served as their constitution. And despite being a small nation dominated by the surrounding empires of Egypt, Assyria, Babylon, Persia, Greece and Rome, they had a sophisticated, even enlightened, legal system. In his 2008 book, *Created Equal: How the Bible Broke with Ancient Political Thought*, Joshua Berman argues that the laws of the Pentateuch were revolutionary within their ancient context as they attempted to establish an egalitarian society.[8] Even the editors of *National Geographic* realized Old Testament laws were progressive at preventing the spread of disease. In their discussion of the recent swine flu global pandemic, they list the laws from the Torah (the Pentateuch) as their earliest example of quarantine.[9]

Yahweh gave a lot of laws, and most of them were obviously good ones. Yahweh commanded the Israelites not to oppress the poor (Ex 23:3, 6; Deut 24:14-15) but to be generous to them (Deut 15:7, 11). Yahweh even commanded his people to help the oxen and donkeys of their enemies (Ex 23:4-5). He not only commanded the Israelites to love him but also to love their neighbors and aliens (Deut 6:5; Lev 19:18, 34). Yahweh commanded them to keep numerous festivals (Ex 23:14-17; Deut 16:1-17), but these feasts were meant to be celebrations, commemorating what he had done for them. It was like God said, "Thou shalt party." God even commanded them to take their tithe and throw a raging party, spending the money on whatever they desired (oxen, sheep, wine or strong drink) and to rejoice before Yahweh their God (Deut 14:22-27). (Remember— God's second command was "Eat a lot of food!") Just to be clear, the Old Testament feasts weren't designed to encourage gluttony but simply to remind Israel that God's generosity was to be celebrated frequently. Just because the Old Testament contains a lot of laws doesn't mean Yahweh is legalistic.

Don't Buy *Sports Illustrated* in Early February

What about all the random laws that don't seem to make any sense? For example, "You shall not wear clothes made of wool and linen woven together" (Deut 22:9-11 NRSV). Why does God care whether or not the Israelites wore clothes that blended wool and linen? Is Yahweh really so high control he wants to tell his people exactly what they can wear? (God should have given a command not to wear stripes with plaids. I would have benefitted from that during my twenties.)

While commands about clothing may seem bizarre and unnecessary, these types of laws are culturally specific, addressing particular problems from their context. Imagine how advice given in a 2010 sermon about lust would sound to a reader in the year 5010: "Don't buy *Sports Illustrated* in early February, and avoid the red-light district." Most males today understand that the *SI* swimsuit issue comes out right after the Super Bowl and that in a certain section of town they can expect to find prostitutes, but in three thousand years (roughly how distant we are from these Old Testament laws) this sound advice for avoiding sexual sin won't make sense. It would seem random, like a command not to wear wool and linen.

Commentators suggest that the wool and linen command might be connected to practices of magic, so an equivalent command might be, "Don't play with a Ouija board," or it may have to do with prostitution, comparable to "Avoid the red-light district."[10] We really don't know what is behind these laws, but since the vast majority of the Old Testament laws make sense and are obviously good laws, it is reasonable to assume that there is a particular societal problem that these types of laws are addressing. Because God is a good lawgiver, he makes laws that are specific enough to deal with contemporary issues and actual circumstances that he knew his people would face.

Get Some Rest

But doesn't the harshness of Yahweh's laws make him seem legalistic? Perhaps, but even laws that seem harsh are given for a good reason. When I asked students in a class for suggestions of problematic Old Testament passages to discuss, several mentioned the story of the guy who gets stoned to death for gathering sticks on the sabbath. Since this incident is tucked away in an obscure section in the book of Numbers, it may be unfamiliar to many readers of the Old Testament.

> While the people of Israel were in the wilderness, they found a man gathering sticks on the Sabbath day. And those who found him gathering sticks brought him to Moses and Aaron and to all the congregation. They put him in custody, because it had not been made clear what should be done to him And the LORD said to Moses, "The man shall be put to death; all the congregation shall stone him with stones outside the camp." And all the congregation brought him outside the camp and stoned him to death with stones, as the LORD commanded Moses. (Num 15:32-36)

What kind of a God would send someone to death for gathering sticks for a fire? This man's actions actually go beyond simple stick gathering, but we first need to look at how Yahweh felt about the sabbath.

The sabbath was important to Yahweh, and he wanted it to be important to his people. It would be difficult to imagine something more important than creating the cosmos, but even while God was doing exactly that, he rested, establishing a precedent for taking a sabbath that goes back to the beginning of time (Gen 2:3). The command to keep the sabbath not only recalled God's creation rest (Ex 20:11; 31:17), it also reminded Israel of their deliverance from Egypt (Deut 5:15). Sabbath was also meant to be a sign of Yahweh's covenant with his people (Ex 31:13, 17). The sabbath was designed to promote justice and limit oppression since slaves could not be forced to work on the sabbath (Ex 20:10; Deut 5:14). Picking up sticks seems harmless, but by doing it on the sabbath the man was denigrating God's creation, his deliverance and his covenant.

Yahweh's punishment for breaking the sabbath also signaled how important the sabbath was. Yahweh not only commanded sabbath rest, he also made it clear both before the golden-calf incident (Ex 31:15) and after it (Ex 35:2-3) that the punishment for violating the sabbath was death. The supposedly innocent stick gatherer would have known that he was committing a crime with a punishment of death. Everyone else knew what he was doing was wrong. His decision to blatantly disobey the word of Yahweh was an act of distrust and rebellion, and Yahweh decided not to be lenient at this point, lest a precedent be set for disobedience. We don't know all of what the man was thinking, but he clearly wasn't trusting God to provide for him. The man's lack of trust in God's provision is shocking, considering he had been supernaturally fed with manna every day since they left Egypt (Ex 16:35).

The timing of the incident is also important. Beforehand, the text narrates the story of the refusal of the people to enter the Promised Land (Num 14) and afterward the rebellion of Korah (Num 16). The time to appear lax about the law was not in the middle of a series of rebellions.

I don't believe the law prescribing death for sabbath breaking is still valid for Christians. As we'll soon see, Jesus didn't support capital punishment for sabbath breaking, but on the sabbath he frequently healed and also allowed his disciples to pluck grain. But the principle of resting and devoting a day to God is still valid. And as we discuss the severity of this punishment, we can't lose sight of the original purpose of the command. The sabbath was meant to be a blessing. Yahweh commanded his people to rest. While a few Old Testament commands might seem random, the command to rest is obviously a good thing.

Many ailments people suffer from today (sports injuries, carpal tunnel syndrome, the common cold, job-related ulcers, stress-induced insomnia, strokes and so on) are caused in part by ignoring the divine mandate to rest. What is often the first thing a doctor tells a sick patient? "Get some rest." God gave that prescription thousands of years ago. Humans know that rest is good, but we still need God to remind us to rest, to command us to rest and occasionally even to punish us when we don't rest.

I'm thankful for the command to rest. Like the commands to reproduce and to eat, it is clearly a command that is meant to bless. I like to tell people, "My God commands me to have sex, eat and rest. Can *your* God beat that?"

In the ancient Babylonian creation myth, *Enuma Elish*, the god Marduk created the humans (from the body of Tiamat, his defeated rival) as slaves to serve the gods so the gods could rest. In the Pentateuch, Yahweh created humans in his own image and then he commanded them to rest in order to bless them. Personally, I prefer Yahweh to Marduk. God's many commands, his specific commands and even his severe commands are all meant to bless his people.

Ordinance Lust?

The psalmist understood that the commands of the Old Testament were meant to be a blessing. When teaching on the psalms, I like to begin class asking the students to complete the sentence (read slowly in an emotional, wispy tone),

My soul is consumed with longing at all times for your . . . what?

Your love? Your lips? Your body? (Lest they go any further, I remind them that our discussion is rated PG, not R.) The psalmist sounds obsessed—but for what? The answer may surprise you. The psalmist's soul was consumed with longing at all times for the *ordinances of Yahweh* (Ps 119:20). Ordinance lust? I may be unique, but I can honestly say that's not something I've experienced.

Readers of the Old Testament may know that Psalm 119 is the longest chapter in the Bible, but they might not realize it is also the longest prayer in the Bible. The whole psalm is addressed directly to God. In each verse, the psalmist tells God that his laws were not only good but also worthy of delight and love. The author of the psalm delights in God's law (Ps 119:14, 16, 24, 35, 47, 70, 77, 92, 143, 176) and loves God's law (Ps 119:47, 97, 113, 119, 127, 132, 159, 163, 165, 167). God's law prompts the psalmist to pant like a dog (Ps 119:131) and to rejoice like one who finds great spoil (Ps 119:162). Most of us have never experienced the finding of plunder, but the language conjures up images we are familiar with—from films of robbers celebrating after a successful heist.

While Danny Ocean and Rusty Ryan (George Clooney and Brad Pitt) are too cool to celebrate their successes in the *Ocean's* films (2001, 2004, 2007), in the third installment (*Ocean's Thirteen*), after Rusty rigs a slot machine to reward the tortured reviewer for the "Five Diamond Award" (David Paymer) with a jackpot of eleven million dollars, the man "rejoices like one who finds great spoil." That is how the psalmist felt about God's commands.

Ultimately, the reason the psalmist loved God's law was not because he was a legalist but because he loved God, and following God's laws brought the psalmist into deeper relationship with God. God's command not to covet (Ex 20:17) was meant to bless the Israelites by freeing them from anxiety over possessions and by making them more dependent on the God who delivered them from Egypt. The commands to have sex, to eat, to rest, to celebrate, to be generous and not to covet were all meant as good gifts from Yahweh to his people. While we may be tempted to think that God wants to burden us with laws and obligations, the author of Psalm 119 knew that his commands were a means of grace and a way for him to bless us.

Jesus Does Good and Saves Life

While some people may perceive a sharp contrast between the graciousness of Jesus and the legalism of Yahweh, Jesus doesn't. He begins his ministry first by quoting from the Old Testament (Mt 4:4, 7, 10), then by explaining how he has not come to abolish the Old Testament law but to fulfill it (Mt 5:17-18). Just like the psalmist, Jesus knows the laws of the Old Testament are good and meant to be a blessing, even particularly the law about the sabbath.[11]

> One **Sabbath** he was going through the grainfields, and as they made their way, his disciples began to pluck heads of grain. And the Pharisees were saying to him, "Look, why are they doing what is not *lawful* on the **Sabbath**?" And he said to them, "Have you never read what David did, when he was in need and was hungry, he and those who were with him: how he entered the house of God, in the time of

Abiathar the high priest, and ate the bread of the Presence, which it is not lawful for any but the priests to eat, and also gave it to those who were with him?" And he said to them, "The **Sabbath** was made for man, not man for the **Sabbath**. So the Son of Man is lord even of the **Sabbath**."

Again he entered the synagogue, and a man was there with a withered hand. And they watched Jesus, to see whether he would heal him on the **Sabbath**, so that they might accuse him. And he said to the man with the withered hand, "Come here." And he said to them, "Is it *lawful* on the **Sabbath** to do good or to do harm, to save life or to kill?" But they were silent. And he looked around at them with anger, grieved at their hardness of heart, and said to the man, "Stretch out your hand." He stretched it out, and his hand was restored. The Pharisees went out and immediately held counsel with the Herodians against him, how to destroy him. (Mk 2:23–3:6)

The Pharisees appear to be concerned about the *sabbath* and upholding the Torah as they point out to Jesus that his own disciples are breaking the sabbath. Jesus' use of the story of David and the holy bread (1 Sam 21:1-9) is problematic, but I'll leave that to a note.[12] Jesus' point is that, just as it was okay for David to break the law to feed his hungry men with the holy bread, it is fine for his disciples to pluck grain on the sabbath to eat. Jesus then claims authority over the sabbath as the Son of Man, declaring that the sabbath law is meant to serve people and not the other way around. The sabbath was designed as a blessing for humans to give them rest and not as a way to deprive them of food (remember, God wants us to eat).

Jesus then enters a synagogue and asks the Pharisees an intriguing question: "Is it *lawful* on the Sabbath to do good or to do harm, to save life or to kill?" Despite appearances, Jesus is concerned about the law. The answer to his question should be obvious. It is lawful to do good and to save life. The Pharisees, however, remain silent. Jesus then proceeds to answer his own question by doing good and saving life. After Jesus heals the man with the withered hand, the Pharisees plot how to destroy him, the first time that Mark tells us they planned to kill Jesus.

Three actions take place on this particular sabbath day: plucking some grain, healing a man and plotting to kill. The disciples pluck. Jesus heals. The Pharisees plot. The Pharisees think it is illegal to pluck and heal on the sabbath, but it is legal to plot murder. Jesus thinks the opposite. He thinks it is okay to pluck, wrong to plot and good to heal. Jesus clearly knows that if he heals the man, they will plan his death (thus ironically breaking the sabbath) from how he frames his question ("to save life or to kill?"), but he still decides to restore the man. I like Jesus' understanding of sabbath better than the Pharisees'.

The sabbath law is meant to guarantee restoration and rest, and Jesus wants to uphold that law for the sake of this man, even though his action will serve as a catalyst for a process that will culminate in his own death. The legalism of the Pharisees lead them to want to deprive the disciples of food, the man of healing and Jesus of life. Jesus is essentially risking his life here to make the point that God's laws are designed to bless people. Jesus is not a legalist and neither is Yahweh.

Avoiding Christian Legalism

So the God of both the Old Testament and the New Testament is not a legalist, but Christians often can be, and to people outside the church those legalisms make God appear legalistic. Christian legalism takes three basic forms.[13] First, God's laws are viewed as a way to earn salvation. It may be tempting to think that the church has moved beyond this issue since the Reformation, but forms of this legalism still thrive today as some churches demand things such as a certain type of baptism, manifestations of spiritual gifts, the avoidance of "bad words," deeds to help the poor or abstinence from alcohol. However, both testaments teach that strict obedience to the law in general or to any specific law cannot make us righteous in God's eyes; only faith in God does that (Gen 15:6; Gal 3:6).

Second, God's laws are viewed as a means to pay God back. When the sermon winds down, the preacher says, "God has done so much for you. He died on the cross for your sins. The least you can do for him is to obey his commands." The problem with this view is that instead of biblical laws being good for us, they are good for God. By obeying his commands, we are somehow doing him a favor. This view sounds more like Marduk in the *Enuma Elish* than Yahweh in the Old Testament or Jesus in the New Testament. Scripture never says we pay God back with our obedience. The cattle on a thousand hills are God's, so if he wants a burger he won't ask us (Ps 50:10-12).[14] The God who made the world and everything in it is not served by human hands as though he needs anything (Acts 17:24-25). While we might not like being in debt, not even to God, we can't pay him back and he doesn't want us to. God's salvation is a gift, pure and simple. No need to pay him back. A "thank you" will suffice— or, better yet, "a sacrifice of thanksgiving" (Ps 50:14).

Third, God's laws are viewed as merely a duty or obligation. No real reason is given for obedience. "God commanded it, I do it." The biggest problem with this form of legalism is that it leads to pride. (I know it's hard to imagine a prideful Christian.) The Bible does provide reasons to obey, because God knows we need motivation.

If we think about helping the poor, for example, we might

find Christians who legalistically say it is necessary to be saved or it is a way to pay God back or it is simply our duty. The Bible gives us plenty of reasons to help the poor, just none of those. God tells us that as we obey his command to help the poor, he blesses us (Deut 15:10; Lk 14:13-14), he hears our prayer (Is 58:7-9), he dwells with us (Jer 7:5-7), we avoid a curse (Prov 28:27), we have treasure in heaven (Mk 10:21) and, my personal favorite, we meet Jesus (Mt 25:34-40). After all, the purpose of the law is to move us deeper into relationship with God. Because God is good, generous and gracious and he wants us to avoid legalism, he provides us with plenty of biblical incentives for following his command to care for the poor—enough incentives to make someone as lazy as me want to go help.

My Little Pharisee

We've all heard stories about Mozart composing at age five or of young prodigies performing complex mathematical calculations in their heads. Well, I was a precocious legalist (I know, it doesn't sound that impressive). When I was in grade school, my mom frequently called me her "little Pharisee." Originally, I didn't know what she meant, but over time I understood. Particularly, when it came to the Bible, I followed the laws and did what I was supposed to do. In high school I was the president of my youth group and was a national all-star in Bible quizzing. (Yes, it's rather pathetic compared to Paul's spiritual CV; Phil 3:4-6.)

When I went off to college, I got involved with InterVarsity and did everything I was supposed to do, attending every possible Bible study, meeting and retreat. At the end of my freshman year, I went on an evangelism project in Boulder, Colorado. One night my staff worker, Greg, invited me to go on a walk, and we ended up sitting in the Buffaloes' football stadium. He asked,

"Why did you come on this evangelism project?"

I wasn't sure what to say: "Because I thought I was supposed to go."

He said, "That's a lousy answer. That sounds like something a Pharisee would say." I told him what my mom called me growing up. We laughed.

I asked, "What would have been a better answer?"

He paused. "If you had said, 'Because God is good and he wants to bless me by making me dependent on him and giving me opportunities to tell others about him.'"

I said, "Yeah, that would have been better."

It would have been better because it's true. Since my conversion from Pharisaism, I've tried to live by the conviction that God is good, generous and gracious, and he gives commands not because he's legalistic but because he wants to bless people and draw them closer into relationship with him.

7

RIGID OR FLEXIBLE?

I was nervous. Fortunately I was next to Shannon. In fact, we were holding hands, but with just our fingertips because the room was sweltering. One of the reasons it was hot was that the building was full of people, mainly friends of ours. The speaker began by saying, "There will be problems because one of you is stubborn." He paused, then tilted his head directly at me.

What? I thought weddings were meant to be encouraging. I guess he thought Shannon needed to be prepared. Shannon thought that the preacher was right that day, and for some unknown reason, after nineteen years of marriage she still thinks I'm stubborn.

Inflexibility Is a Good Thing?

Have you ever heard someone say, "Oh, I love that guy! He's so stubborn. In fact, he's so inflexible, he never changes his mind." There's no doubt that being stubborn is valuable in certain contexts. It was good that the Allied troops on D-Day stubbornly persisted despite early heavy losses on the Normandy beaches. But it is difficult to imagine a rigid person as being perceived positively. People generally don't want to be described as stubborn or inflexible. Most of us have had a negative experience of working closely with someone who has fixed views and dogmatically enlightens others of the "truth." She or he is not the type of person you invite to your book club. (I've never been invited to a book club. Hmm . . .)

While the U.S. TV show *The Office* is full of quirky characters, the one most characterized by stubbornness is Angela Martin, head of accounting and the authoritarian ruler of The Party Planning Committee (a.k.a. The PPC). In the Old Testament, the ability to be flexible and the ability to forgive are related, and apparently this correlation is also true in *The Office*. Angela is so inflexible she can't forgive Dwight for euthanizing her sick cat. (Dwight was stupid, but he thought he was putting the cat out of her misery. The lethal dose of Benadryl he administered didn't do the trick, so he put Sprinkles in the freezer, where she finally met her demise.[1]) Sadly, but not surprisingly, Angela also happens to be a devout Christian. No one likes to be around an inflexible person like Angela.

When Christians speak about God, however, his immutability or lack of changing is considered a good thing, based on how frequently the topic is mentioned. Ministers from certain theological traditions love to preach about God's immutability. Despite the fact that God's immutability would normally seem a topic relegated to the ranks of academic theologians (my spell-checker does not consider "unchangeability" a word), numerous popular worship songs sing the praises of our "Almighty, Unchangeable God."[2]

But for those of us who have felt bullied, cajoled or humiliated by inflexible people, sermons and choruses that praise God's unchangeability might seem oxymoronic. How did inflexibility become a good thing?

The Unchangeable God of the Old Testament

A discussion of relevant biblical texts will hopefully shed some light on this question. While a few New Testament texts portray God as unchangeable (Jas 1:17), the texts used most frequently to support the doctrine of God's immutability are found in the Old Testament. Specifically, four texts are mentioned repeatedly: Numbers 23:19; 1 Samuel 15:29; Psalms 110:4; and Malachi 3:6. It appears that this divine attribute is more of an Old Testament than a New Testament phenomenon. God's inflexibility could, therefore, be considered to be consistent with other negative characteristics of Yahweh as portrayed in the Old Testament. In the spirit of Marcionite thinking, the God that sometimes appears to be angry, sexist and racist could also be described as rigid, stubborn and inflexible.

While some of us may not like the fact that the God of the Old Testament is described as unchangeable, since that is what the Bible says, perhaps we just need to accept it. God's immutability is just one of those biblical doctrines that we need to swallow, even if it feels like a bitter pill. As we start looking at specific passages, we are going to find that God's commitment to not change is actually a very good thing.

Changing, Relenting and Repenting

If there is one Hebrew word that the issue of divine changeability centers on, it would be *naham*, since it is used in most of the references describing God either changing or not changing his mind.[3] The root *naham* has three basic meanings: (1) to *change one's mind*, (2) to *regret* and (3) to *show compassion*. The context usually makes it clear whether *naham* is referring to a mind change, to regret or to compassion. Here I will focus on texts that fit the first meaning, because changing one's mind implies mutability or flexibility (the sidebar at the end of this chapter summarizes these references).[4]

English versions still translate *naham* slightly differently in contexts in which a divine change of mind is involved. For example, in Exodus 32:14, older translations inform us that Yahweh "repented" (KJV, RSV), but since repentance is often associated with sin and God is without sin, this statement could be controversial.[5] We don't want to suggest that Yahweh needed to repent for his sins (or we might get struck by lightning; see chapter two).

More modern translations of Exodus 32:14 tell us that Yahweh either "changed his mind" (NAS, NRSV) or "relented" (NIV, ESV, TNIV). While most of us don't use the word *relent* often, it simply means to change one's mind, particularly away from a harsh decision. Interestingly, the Latin root from which *relent* is derived, *lentus*, means flexible. So, a person or a God who relents is flexible. Regardless of whether the English translation for *naham* mentions change, relenting or repenting, each of these words implies flexibility or mutability. Now we can look at the relevant *naham* passages.

Unwaveringly Committed to Doing Good

In the Old Testament it is good news that Yahweh doesn't change, because that means his blessing on his people will continue. Of the four primary Old Testament texts that mention divine immutability, three of them use the verb *naham*, each time with a negative participle, stating basically that God does not change. Balaam declares to Balak, ruler of Moab, that since Yahweh has promised to bless Israel, he would not change his mind (*naham*) and curse them instead (Num 23:19). Samuel tells Saul that Yahweh is not like a man that he should change his mind (*naham*) regarding the judgment to tear the kingdom away from Saul and give it to his neighbor David (1 Sam 15:29).

The psalmist explains that Yahweh will not change his mind (*naham*) about his decision to make the addressee a priest forever, in the order of Melchizedek (Ps 110:4). The one text where *naham* isn't used is found in the book of Malachi, specifically in an oracle in which Yahweh states that he does not change (*shanah*), and therefore Israel has not perished (Mal 3:6).

In three of the four texts, the divine immutability involves a promise or commitment by Yahweh to bless his people. In Numbers, Moab will not be allowed to defeat Israel, in Psalms the messianic individual will not be removed from the priesthood, and in Malachi Israel will not perish. If God were to have changed his mind in these three contexts, negative repercussions would have resulted for his people.

The fourth text, the judgment against Saul, includes a promise to bless David, Saul's neighbor. Because Saul is being removed from power, David will become king. Therefore, for the people in these texts, except Saul, Yahweh's lack of flexibility is a positive thing.[6] The point of these passages is that Yahweh will not change his mind about blessing his people. In these situations, flexibility would have resulted in judgment and death, but divine rigidness results in mercy and life. Thus divine "stubbornness" is good in these contexts.

The main point that these texts are making is not simply that God is unchangeable, but that God is unchangeable about his commitment to bless his people. And those additional words make a huge difference in how the message of divine immutability comes across. Unchangeability is not necessarily a valuable end by itself, and in certain contexts it would be bad, as we will see. What makes it good is that God is unwaveringly committed to doing good. That is something I personally find praiseworthy. (I'd write a song about it, but people probably wouldn't want to sing it.)

An Expanded Bucket List

However, the issue of God's immutability is a little more complicated than some preachers might have us think, since the Bible also describes God as changeable.[7] Hezekiah was not only a righteous ruler of Judah, he was also one of many Old Testament individuals who changed the mind of Yahweh.

> In those days Hezekiah became sick and was at the point of death. And Isaiah the prophet the son of Amoz came to him and said to him, "Thus says the LORD, 'Set your house in order, for you shall die; you shall not recover.'" Then Hezekiah turned his face to the wall and *prayed* to the LORD, saying, "Now, O LORD, please remember how I have walked before you in faithfulness and with a whole heart, and have done what is good in your sight." And Hezekiah wept bitterly. And before Isaiah had gone out of the middle court, the word of the LORD came to him: "Turn back, and say to Hezekiah the leader of my people, Thus says the LORD, the God of David your father: I have heard your *prayer*; I have seen your tears. Behold, I will heal you. On the third day you shall go up to the house of the LORD, and I will add fifteen years to your life. I will deliver you and this city out of the hand of the king of Assyria, and I will defend this city for my own sake and for my servant David's sake." (2 Kings 20:1-6)

Hezekiah is sick, on his deathbed. The prophet Isaiah delivers the message from Yahweh that Hezekiah is going to die. Just in case the message wasn't clear, Isaiah repeats it: "You shall not recover." While this word seems harsh, it wasn't a punishment, and it gave Hezekiah an opportunity to prepare for the inevitable. Hezekiah, however, isn't content to just "put his house in order," so he *prays*, laying out his spiritual CV. But interestingly he never tells Yahweh what to do. He also broke down, literally: "he wept a great weeping." Suddenly, Yahweh tells Isaiah to return to the king and inform him he will live for fifteen more years. If I were Isaiah, I would interrupt Yahweh at this point and say, "God, you can't change your mind about this. It's going to make us both look indecisive and weak."[8] Fortunately for Hezekiah, Isaiah was not like me.

Lest we think that Yahweh only appeared to change his mind, the text makes the divine change explicit. At first, Yahweh and Isaiah were in agreement that Hezekiah's death was definite and imminent. He was at death's door. His bucket list would fit on a postage stamp.[9] In Isaiah's second message, however, Yahweh states that he will heal Hezekiah and add fifteen years to his life. Hezekiah's new, expanded bucket list will include defeating perhaps the most powerful man on the planet, Sennacherib, ruler of the Assyrian Empire (that sounds better than skydiving).

What caused the change in Yahweh? Prayer and tears. Yahweh explained that he changed his mind because he had heard Hezekiah's prayer and had seen Hezekiah's tears. While the verb *naham* isn't used in this Hezekiah passage, the book of Jeremiah mentions a similar incident from Hezekiah's life and uses the word, describing how Yahweh changed his mind (*naham*) after Hezekiah prayed (Jer 26:19). Prayer is effective. I have difficultly motivating myself to pray, but stories like this provide a powerful incentive.

Changing the Mind of God

Was this flexible behavior of Yahweh toward Hezekiah typical or unusual? While four Old Testament texts state Yahweh does not change, many more describe Yahweh as changing his mind (see sidebar at the end of this chapter). Problematically, the same verb *naham* is used in most of these other passages to describe Yahweh as changing. Since this type of divine behavior is often ignored by teachers of the Bible, I will include many Old Testament passages in which Yahweh changes, to emphasize that this isn't just a minor or obscure Old Testament topic but actually a major aspect of God's character. If you are tempted to skip to the next section, don't, because it is important to see how and why Yahweh changes.

In general, Yahweh changes in the context of showing compassion toward his people, often responding to human intercession, as he did for Hezekiah. Moses changes the mind of God, not once but twice. After Israel worshiped the golden calf, Moses interceded, almost as if he were using peer pressure ("What Would the Egyptians Say?"), so Yahweh relented (*naham*) from destroying his people (Ex 32:12, 14). After the Israelites refused to enter the land, based on the report of the twelve spies, Yahweh initially declared he would strike all the Israelites and disinherit them and start over with Moses, but then he changed his mind (*naham* is not used), after Moses' request for mercy (Num 14:11-20). (If I were Moses, I would have agreed with Yahweh's initial proposal. "Sure, let's start over with just me.")

In response to David's assertion about the greatness of his mercy, Yahweh relented (*naham*) concerning the pestilence he had sent upon Israel for David's census and therefore interrupted the punishment (2 Sam 24:16; 1 Chron 21:15). The psalmist describes a period when Yahweh heard the cry of his oppressed people and remembered his covenant, so he relented (*naham*)[10] according to his steadfast love (Ps 106:44-45). While the books of Exodus and Samuel narrate specific incidents of divine mutability, this psalm describes a broader pattern or a general characteristic of Yahweh as a God who relents, which could fit easily into the cycles of the book of Judges.

Bovine Contrition

The theme of divine changeability occurs most frequently in prophetic literature, particularly in Jeremiah.[11] If you want to see all the places Yahweh changes his mind just in the book of Jeremiah, check out this long note.[12] Apparently, Yahweh changed his mind so often regarding potential judgments against Israel that Jeremiah reported that Yahweh complained of being weary of relenting (*naham*) (Jer 15:6).

The Minor Prophets also speak of how God changed his mind regarding punishments he had intended to mete out. In a series of four visions, Yahweh first showed the prophet Amos what type of judgment he was about to perform against Israel, but then in response to Amos's desperate pleas for mercy after the first two visions (locusts and fire), Yahweh twice relented (*naham*) and declared the punishment would not happen (Amos 7:1-3, 4-6). In Joel's description of Yahweh's attributes, along with graciousness, mercifulness and slowness to anger, Yahweh is said to relent (*naham*) from punishing (Joel 2:12-14).

In the book of Jonah, after all the Ninevites repented (even the animals wore sackcloth), God changed his mind (*naham*) about the evil that he had said he would bring on them and he did not do it (Jon 3:8-10). Jonah was not surprised, because he knew that God is gracious, merciful, abounding in love and ready to relent (*naham*) from punishing (Jon 4:2). Thus, according to both Joel and Jonah, Yahweh's willingness to change his mind to show mercy wasn't just a capricious whim, but it characterized his nature. God was concerned about all the Ninevites, and even their cattle (bovine contrition always helps).[13]

Divine changeability is precisely what infuriated Jonah so much, because he wanted Nineveh to be destroyed. Jonah perceived God's willingness to move from judgment to mercy as a weakness, while Joel saw it as a strength. I guess it depends on your perspective whether or not divine flexibility is a good thing. Yahweh's flexibility was good for Hezekiah as well as for many other people in the Old Testament.

So, the Bible seems to say both that God changes and that he doesn't change. Which one is it? Is God flexible or not?

Ignore, Rationalize or Work to Understand

To reconcile these apparently contradictory aspects of God's character, we have three options before us. First, we can ignore one of these characteristics. Depending on our theological tradition, we simply teach the texts that stress the aspect of God's character that we are comfortable with (either God's immutability or his mutability). In his argument for divine immutability, Thomas Aquinas quoted Malachi 3:6 as well as Augustine, Plato and Dionysius.[14] I can excuse Aquinas for not mentioning the three other Old Testament texts that mention divine immutability, since unlike me, he probably wasn't using BibleWorks 7.0 (perhaps an earlier version?). But it is hard to imagine that the greatest scholastic theologian was unaware of all the passages in which God changes his mind, since several of them come from familiar stories like Exodus 32 and Jonah 3. He appears to ignore those texts because they don't fit his theology.

In his argument for an open view of God, Richard Rice doesn't completely ignore Old Testament texts that speak of divine immutability, but he mentions only two (Num 23:19; 1 Sam 15:29) and then ignores the two others discussed above (Mal 3:6; Ps 110:4).[15] If Rice were to mention only these two, it wouldn't be so bad, but he specifically contrasts the "two passages" where "God does not repent" with the "forty or so indicating that he does."[16] Rice's point that there are far more texts speaking of divine mutability than immutability is still valid, but like Aquinas, he seems to be ignoring relevant texts.[17]

Second, we can rationalize that even though Scripture describes God as both mutable and immutable, he is actually only one of them. In his sermon titled "The Most High, a Prayer-Hearing God," Jonathan Edwards argues that in Exodus 32:14 God does not actually change his mind but just appears to change his mind.[18] While overall the sermon is inspiring and motivates one to pray, at this point Edwards distorts the straightforward meaning of the text: Yahweh says he will destroy Israel, Moses asks Yahweh not to destroy them, and so Yahweh changes his mind and forgives them. If the text tells us that God changed his mind, but we conclude that that couldn't have happened because we know (from Aquinas?) God can't change, then we have a problem. If Exodus 32:14 were the only place that Yahweh changed his mind, then Edward's argument would carry more weight, but as we've seen already, that is simply not the case. God changes his mind frequently in the Old Testament. When our systematic theology comes into conflict with the Bible, the former needs to be modified, not the latter.

Third, we can work to understand how these two apparently contradictory yet biblical descriptions of God can be faithfully reconciled without downplaying the tensions. (In case you weren't sure, this is the option I recommend.) We hold them in tension and avoid attempts to overly systematize the Bible.

Predictably Flexible, Constantly Changeable and Immutably Mutable

One way these tensions are often understood is to say that God's character does not change, but his judgments do.[19] Generally, I agree with this idea. However, I don't think it is the most helpful way to explain the problem. By focusing on the difference between God's unchanging character and his changing judgments, a distinction is set up that Scripture simply doesn't make. The problem goes beyond just the Bible never stating something like "God's character doesn't change, but his judgments do." Since the same verb *naham* is used to inform us both that Yahweh has changed and that he doesn't change, it is difficult to argue that in certain passages *naham* clearly refers to his unchanging character and in other passages it clearly refers to his decisions, which may change.

However, if we look at patterns among the relevant passages, we see that the text consistently portrays God as unchangeable in certain contexts and as changeable in other contexts. The context is, therefore, crucial if we want to understand this apparent biblical paradox.

In contexts where there is doubt as to whether or not God will be faithful, the text declares that he does not waver from his commitments. Yahweh has promised to bless his people, so he won't suddenly start to curse them (Num 23:19-20). Since Yahweh does not change, his people Israel have not perished (Mal 3:6). It's not simply that God doesn't ever change, but specifically that he doesn't change regarding his promises to his covenant people.

In contexts of imminent judgment from God, when people repent, he changes his mind and shows mercy. Not only did Yahweh change to show mercy to his people the Israelites but he also did it for Gentiles, specifically the Ninevites (he is, after all, not racist; see chapter four). Yahweh listened and showed compassion based on the intercession of both rulers (Hezekiah) and prophets (Amos).[20] The text includes both specific incidents of Yahweh changing from judgment to forgiveness (Num 14:20; Jer 26:19) and general descriptions of Yahweh being eager to relent and show mercy (Jon 4:2) and as remembering his covenant and showing compassion (Ps 106:44-45). It's not that

God always changes and is inconsistent, but specifically in situations where people deserve punishment, when they repent, he consistently changes from judgment to grace.

For anyone worried about the orthodoxy of this discussion because it goes against what you've been taught, remember that a focus on context is ultimately a focus on God's Word. Unfortunately, a narrow, proof-texting approach to the Bible often characterizes discussions or sermons on this topic, which can easily distort the broader message of the text. We can't simply base our theological conclusions on one statement God speaks in isolation, but we need to see what he is doing more generally whenever he makes a particular statement. When we approach Scripture, we must take the context seriously.

As we look at the contexts of these passages, we see not a divine contradiction but a consistent pattern. The Old Testament characters themselves understood both the changing and the unchanging aspect of God's nature. Moses, David, Hezekiah, the psalmist, Jeremiah, Amos, Joel and Jonah all knew that the flexible aspect of Yahweh's character does not change. According to the Old Testament, God is predictably flexible, constantly changeable and immutably mutable, at least in regard to showing mercy toward repentant sinners.

Jesus and the Female "Dog"

Not surprisingly, Jesus also displays compassionate flexibility during his ministry. While he spent most of his time in the region of Galilee, on one occasion he travels further north to the region of Tyre, where he encounters a Gentile woman from Syrophoenicia.

> And from there he arose and went away to the region of Tyre and Sidon. And he entered a house and did not want

anyone to know, yet he could not be hidden. But immediately a woman whose little *daughter* had an unclean spirit heard of him and came and fell down at his feet. Now the woman was a Gentile, a Syrophoenician by birth. And she begged him to cast the demon out of her *daughter.* And he said to her, "Let the children be fed first, for it is not right to take the children's bread and throw it to the **dogs**." But she answered him, "Yes, Lord; yet even the **dogs** under the table eat the children's crumbs." And he said to her, "For this statement you may go your way; the demon has left your *daughter.*" And she went home and found the child lying in bed and the demon gone. (Mk 7:24-30)

The woman asks Jesus to cast a demon out of her *daughter,* a task he has done numerous times elsewhere, so one would expect him to agree. Shockingly, he tells her, "Let the children be fed first, for it is not right to take the children's bread and throw it to the *dogs*." In Jesus' analogy, the children are the Jews and the dogs are the Gentiles. So, to grant her request would be like giving Jewish "bread" to a Gentile "dog." Yes, he does essentially call her a female dog, which would have had worse connotations in Jesus' day than it has in ours.[21]

I have never had the privilege to be personally insulted by Jesus, but when others insult me, I don't respond well (perhaps I'm unusual in this regard?). Amazingly, the Syrophoenician woman doesn't seem to take offense at being called a dog. She even makes a brilliant response using the language of Jesus' analogy: But even the dogs get crumbs from under the table. She realizes that even if she does not deserve to sit down at the table yet, the crumbs from Jesus' table will be sufficient. (Presumably, she envisioned a table with young children.) She understood that Jesus had ample power to heal both Jews and

Gentiles, so an exorcism of her daughter should be no problem for him.

Jesus then replies that because of her response, her daughter has already been healed. He is not going to heal her daughter initially, but after his interaction with the woman he agrees to do it. One could argue that he was planning on helping her all along, but that is not what the passage says. Jesus makes it explicit that he healed the girl because of the woman's statement. He was not planning to help her initially. While I am still troubled by what Jesus says to the woman—it almost sounds racist—his actions speak louder than his words. The woman clearly wasn't bothered by Jesus' comments, but both she and her daughter were clearly blessed by his healing.

When Does God Change or Not Change in the Old Testament?

The Old Testament references below use the Hebrew verb *naham* (except Num 14:20 and Mal 3:6), which has three primary meanings:

1. To *relent,* repent or change one's mind. The references below fit this meaning.

2. To *regret* or feel sorry. Yahweh regrets making the humans (Gen 6:6, 7).

3. To *comfort* or show compassion. Yahweh will comfort Zion (Zech 1:17).

God does not change. He is faithful, consistent and dependable. There are four divine immutability Old Testament references:

1. Balak of Moab tries to force Balaam to make Yahweh curse Israel,

but Yahweh has promised to bless Israel, so he *won't change* and curse them (Num 23:19).

2. Yahweh *won't change* his mind about removing Saul from the throne (1 Sam 15:29). But the context also says Yahweh regretted (*naham*) making Saul king (1 Sam 15:11, 35).

3. Yahweh *won't change* and remove the messianic figure from the priesthood (Ps 110:4).

4. Yahweh *doesn't change*, so Israel has not perished (Mal 3:6).

God changes. He is merciful, compassionate and gracious. There are sixteen divine mutability Old Testament references:

1. Twice Moses intercedes and Yahweh *relents*, so the judgment against his people is reduced (Ex 32:14; Num 14:20).

2. David's census. Yahweh *relents* and stops the pestilence (2 Sam 24:16; 1 Chron 21:15).

3. Yahweh heard the cry of his people and *relented* according to his *hesed* (Ps 106:45).

4. Yahweh *relents* so much he gets tired of it (Jer 15:6). Yahweh may *relent* and not do good to his people (Jer 18:10). Yahweh will *relent* if they repent (Jer 26:3, 13). Hezekiah's prayer *changed* Yahweh's mind (Jer 26:19; compare 2 Kings 20:1-6; Is 38:1-6). If they obey, Yahweh will *relent* from the judgment he had brought on them (Jer 42:10).

5. Twice Amos intercedes and Yahweh *relents* of the judgments of locusts and fire on Israel (Amos 7:3, 6).

6. Yahweh is characterized as gracious, slow to anger and *relenting* from punishment (Joel 2:13-14).

7. Yahweh *relents* from judgment on Nineveh (Jon 3:10). Jonah knows that Yahweh is characterized by *relenting* from judgment (Jon 4:2).

While this story may seem strange, it shouldn't strike us as odd that Jesus would change his mind to show compassion, because as we've seen throughout the Old Testament, God is both loyal toward his commitments and flexible when it comes to showing mercy. The Syrophoenician woman and her daughter were both glad Jesus wasn't completely unchangeable but, instead, was flexible.

The Flexible and Unchanging God

Is it good that God changes his mind? To Jonah, it was not good that Yahweh changed his mind. Jonah wanted the wicked Assyrians to be destroyed. But if you were a Ninevite, an Israelite, Hezekiah or David, it was good that Yahweh changed his mind. If you are a child who deserves to be punished, it is good when a parent changes his mind about your punishment. If you are a car buyer, it is bad when a used-car dealer changes his mind about the low price he had promised.

The fact that God doesn't change his commitments but remains faithful to his promises is great news, but the fact that he extends not condemnation but mercy to the contrite is even greater news. Wouldn't it also be great if Christians had a reputation of being like God in this way and not like inflexible Angela from *The Office*, if we were known as being unchangeable in a good way (faithful, loyal, reliable and dependable) and changeable in a good way (merciful, gracious, flexible and compassionate). To make this true, Christians will need to teach not only about divine immutability but also about divine flexibility.

When I was eight I went to a church summer camp for the first time. I have three memories from that camp, one bad and two good. First, I discovered a nine-year-old girl liked me (that's bad). Second, we snuck a garter snake into the girl's cabin (that's good). Third, I committed my life to Jesus (that's very good).

On the final night, the speaker told us that people who didn't have a relationship with Jesus would go to hell. (I wouldn't generally recommend this method of evangelism, but it worked for me when I was eight.) I didn't want to go to hell. I've always been motivated more by the pitchfork than the carrot. I raised my hand and prayed the prayer. Just like the Ninevites, I repented and God relented from meting out the future judgment I deserved.

I think it was good that God changed his assessment of me. I also think it is good that I can know he will not change his promises to be faithful to me. It is also good that I am stubborn, because it means I won't change my deep commitments to Shannon and to Jesus.

8

DISTANT OR NEAR?

Well, where is God . . . if he's alive? And why doesn't he speak anymore?"[1]

Mrs. Coulter asks these questions to a minister of the church in *The Amber Spyglass* by British novelist Philip Pullman. The book is the third in the *His Dark Materials* series, written as a sort of Chronicles of Narnia for atheists.[2] While it might be tempting for Christians to criticize the cynical view of God expressed by Pullman's book—or specifically by Mrs. Coulter's character (played by Nicole Kidman in the 2007 film *The Golden Compass*)—similar perspectives are found in the Old Testament. Many people in the Old Testament ask where the God of Israel is (2 Kings 2:14; Ps 42:3, 10; 79:10; 115:2; Joel 2:17; Mic 7:10; Mal 2:17). The psalmist frequently speaks of God being far away (Ps 10:1; 35:22; 38:21; 71:12). The author of Psalm 22 asks God directly why he is so distant:

> My **God**, my **God**, *why* have you forsaken me?
> *Why* are you so far from saving me, from the words of my groaning?

O my God, I cry by day, but you do not answer,
and by night, but I find no rest. (Ps 22:1-2)

Many of us may resonate with these questions and feelings. In the midst of a personal crisis, we wonder where God is. God is remote, so along with the psalmist we ask, "Where are you God?" While he was hanging on a cross, Jesus quoted Psalm 22, exclaiming, "My God, my God, why have you forsaken me?" (Mt 27:46; Mk 15:34). Even God's Son asks his father why he has deserted him. When Jesus needed to express this sentiment, he went to the Old Testament. The God of the Old Testament seems to be distant.

And yet the God of the Old Testament is also near. Every Christmas we are reminded that one of Jesus' names is "God is with us" (Immanuel; Mt 1:23), but it is easy to forget that this particular messianic title first appears in the Old Testament when it was given as part of a divine promise to an eighth-century king, Ahaz (Is 7:14).[3] In fact, the idea of God being present with his people is found all over the Old Testament. God was not only with specific individuals (patriarchs, judges, kings and prophets), but also with his people generally. Yahweh communicates his presence to his people in many ways, some of them quite surprising.

Those Miserable Psalms

In the film *Monty Python and the Holy Grail* (1975), "God" speaks as a head in the clouds (no, this isn't what I just meant by surprising), calling Arthur to seek the grail.

God: Arthur! Arthur, King of the Britons! Oh, don't grovel! If there's one thing I can't stand, it's people groveling.

Arthur: Sorry—

> God: And don't apologize. Every time I try to talk to
> someone it's "sorry this" and "forgive me that"
> and "I'm not worthy." What are you doing now?
> Arthur: I'm averting my eyes, O Lord.
> God: Well, don't. It's like **those miserable psalms**—
> they're so depressing.

While we might resonate with the Python-esque negative
perspective about the whininess of certain psalms, the real God
is fortunately not offended by honest feelings, thoughts and
questions.[4] And as we look at one of "those miserable psalms,"
more frequently called laments, we learn profound lessons
about being in relationship to God.

Psalm 13 begins a bit like Psalm 22, with questions about
God's absence.

> [1] **How long**, O LORD? Will you forget me *forever?*
> **How long** will you hide your face from me?
> [2] **How long** must I take counsel in my soul and have sorrow
> in my heart *all the day?*
> **How long** shall my enemy be exalted over me?
> [3] Consider and answer me, O LORD my God;
> light up my eyes, lest I sleep the sleep of death,
> [4] lest my enemy say, "I have prevailed over him,"
> lest my foes rejoice because I am shaken.
> [5] But I have trusted in your steadfast love;
> my heart shall rejoice in your salvation.
> [6] I will sing to the LORD,
> because he has dealt bountifully with me. (Ps 13)

The psalmist is in pain and feels cut off from God. This isolation has been going on "*forever*," prompting the fourfold repeti-

tion of "How long?" The psalmist is forgotten, but Yahweh is
hidden. Death is near, but Yahweh is far. The psalmist is desperate, but Yahweh is distant. Yahweh is once again absent from
a person in crisis.

However, after verse 2 the tone of the psalm changes from
questioning and despair to petition and finally to trust and
praise. It is hard to imagine how the pessimist of verses 1-2
becomes the optimist of verses 5-6. What happened? Is the
psalmist bipolar? To understand this, it is helpful to compare
Psalm 13 to other psalms of lament. Psalm 13 actually follows
the basic pattern for a lament, typically consisting of five parts:
(1) *invocation*, "O LORD"; (2) *complaint*, "Will you forget me forever?"; (3) *petition,* "Consider and answer me"; (4) *trust,* "I have
trusted"; and (5) *praise,* "I will sing."[5]

While the confidence and trust of the psalmist is obvious by
the end, ironically even in the despondent questions at the beginning we find a kernel of faith that God is still present. If
Yahweh were completely absent, why would the psalmist even
bother to speak to him? God seems hidden, but at least the
conversation is still going on. The psalmist addresses God directly in verses 1, 3 and 5, calling him Yahweh ("O LORD") and
using second-person pronouns. The honest expression of despair over God's absence eventually helps move the person back
to a place of trust and praise.

Why Is This Psalm in the Bible?

Perhaps the most surprising thing about this psalm is that it is
included in the Bible at all. Since laments could make God look
bad because he appears to forsake (Ps 22) and forget (Ps 13) his
people, we might think God would be offended by them just
like Monty Python's God in the clouds. But if God were really
offended, he shouldn't have inspired so many laments and au-

thorized their inclusion in his Word.[6] Laments are by far the most common type of psalm; over 40 percent of the psalms are laments.[7] However, they are also the most frequently ignored type of psalm.

God apparently thought it was good for the writers of Scripture to express their honest questions about his apparent absence. God gave laments to his people as a way to pray in the midst of pain. Jesus even modeled appropriate use of a lament (Ps 22) by showing how relevant it was to his own crisis as he was dying on a cross. However, the primary reason Jesus quoted Psalm 22 wasn't to model how to lament and it wasn't to show how a messianic psalm pointed to him. He quoted Psalm 22 because it expressed what he was feeling. He needed to lament. And so do we.

When God seems distant in the midst of crises and pain, we can pray the psalms of lament. As we follow the pattern of the lament—from doubts and despair to prayer and petition—we eventually arrive at a place of hope, trust and praise. While it happens quickly in the six verses of Psalm 13, it may take much longer in our own lives. But there are plenty of psalms of lament to read during times of trouble. God knows that there will be times when he feels distant from us, so during those times he has provided prayers, these "miserable psalms" of lament that not only keep the communication lines open but also gradually draw us back into his presence, into a place of trust and faith.

Oxford Was Trying to Get Rid of Me

While I was trying to get my doctorate in Old Testament, at several points in my program I wanted to quit. The lowest point came two years into the program after my master's exams, which should have resulted in my promotion to doctoral status, but instead Oxford said I needed to remain as a master's student to possibly obtain yet another master's degree (I had three already), an M.Litt., which is like the consolation prize for people who don't achieve a D.Phil. (Oxford's version of a Ph.D.). It felt like Oxford was trying to get rid of me. Also, in a few weeks I would head back to the United States for a college reunion, not exactly the best time to be in the middle of a professional crisis. I had just turned forty, and my hopes for the future were being crushed.

One afternoon, I took a long walk along the canal in Oxford and lamented. I vented my frustration at God, asking him why this was happening to me, how long this would go on and where he was. While I didn't receive any clear divine response immediately, afterward I felt better. The act of lamenting was cathartic. However, over the course of the summer, God manifested his presence to me through colleagues, friends and family who encouraged me to persevere. Three years later, I got my D.Phil.

You Shouldn't Talk Like That

When I teach on lament psalms, I ask the class, "What might a Christian today say if he or she saw another Christian hanging on a cross uttering these words: 'My God, my God, why have you forsaken me?'" Typical answers follow:

> "You shouldn't talk like that. The book of Romans tells us that nothing can separate us from the love of God."

> "Don't be so discouraged. Gabriel told Mary that nothing is impossible with God."

> "It can't be that bad. The prophet Jeremiah tells you that God knows the plans he has for you, plans for your welfare, not for harm."[8]

We are good at quoting "happy" passages at people who are

in pain. But when Jesus was on the cross, he didn't focus on a hopeful psalm or song ("Always look on the bright side of life . . .") but on a lament. If Jesus lamented, maybe we should too.

When I first came to my seminary, I met James,[9] a new student who shared with me about the struggles he and his wife had in their efforts to become parents. They had tried for several years to conceive and finally became pregnant. Just two months before I met James, his wife had miscarried while in her first trimester. They were in the midst of grief but were torn because somehow it didn't seem right for Christians to complain. James said, "But God is good, and I shouldn't complain." I didn't know what to say, so I didn't say anything for a while.

Eventually I said, "I think you should complain. The psalmist complained." (I should have added, "And even Jesus lamented.") We prayed that God would help them grieve and lament their loss and also that God would bless them with a child someday. Later, when James took my psalms class, he wrote his own psalm of lament about the miscarriage. About two years after our initial conversation and prayer, I rejoiced with him when his son was born.

There Are Some Who Call Me . . . Yahweh

While the authors of Psalms 13 and 22 wanted God to be close, the people of Israel at the foot of Mount Sinai wanted him to be distant.

> Then Moses brought the people out of the camp *to meet God*, and they took their stand at the foot of the mountain. Now Mount Sinai was wrapped in smoke because the LORD had descended on it in fire. The smoke of it went up like the smoke of a kiln, and the whole mountain trembled greatly. And as the sound of the trumpet grew louder and

louder, Moses spoke, and God answered him in thunder. The LORD came down on Mount Sinai, to the top of the mountain. And the LORD called Moses to the top of the mountain, and Moses went up.

And the LORD said to Moses, "Go down and warn the people, lest they break through to the LORD to look and many of them perish. Also let the priests who *come near to the* LORD consecrate themselves, lest the LORD break out against them." And Moses said to the LORD, "The people cannot come up to Mount Sinai, for you yourself warned us, saying, 'Set limits around the mountain and consecrate it.'" And the LORD said to him, "Go down, and come up bringing Aaron with you. But do not let the priests and the people break through to come up to the LORD, lest he break out against them." So Moses went down to the people and told them. . . .

Now when all the people saw the thunder and the flashes of lightning and the sound of the trumpet and the mountain smoking, the people were afraid and trembled, and **they stood far off** and said to Moses, "You speak to us, and we will listen; but do not let God speak to us, lest we die." Moses said to the people, "Do not fear, for God has come to test you, that the fear of him may be before you, that you may not sin." **The people stood far off,** while Moses *drew near to the thick darkness where God was.* (Ex 19:17-25; 20:18-21)

There are several reasons why the Israelites don't want to be close to God. Yahweh's behavior in this passage is intimidating, with all the lightning, thunder, smoke and explosions (reminiscent of the enchanter Tim in *The Holy Grail*). Who would want to get close to all that fire and noise?

Yahweh does distance himself here from his people, but he does it for a purpose. He has just delivered them from Egyptian bondage, and lest they think he will protect them no matter how they behave, he wants them to revere him, particularly as he delivers the Ten Commandments (Ex 20:1-17). They need to understand that he is holy, powerful and concerned about obedience.

But in this incident, even as Yahweh is loud and frightful, he is also near and tangible. At the beginning of the passage, Moses brings the people out of their camp for the purpose of meeting God. God doesn't allow them to come close, but there's a good reason for that: he's trying to protect them from harm (I'll discuss this idea more in the next section). And yet they still meet him, even though it may not have been what they expected. They see the lightning, hear the thunder, smell the smoke and feel the earthquake. All these manifestations of power are signs to them that God is real, present and close. They experience God.

While the people need to stand far off, the person that knows God best, Moses, wants to draw near to God. Moses has already experienced several theophanies (divine encounters), the most famous of which was at the burning bush (Ex 3:2). Moses would have been afraid of the divine thunder and fire like everyone else, but he knows that the risk is worth it to be in the presence of Yahweh. At Mount Sinai, Yahweh is both distant and close to his people. Moses values the presence of God so much that shortly after this incident he argues with God to convince him not to leave. Let's look at that next.

Should He Stay or Should He Go?

Everything is going well until God's people make the golden calf and worship it (Ex 32:1-6), breaking the first two commands that God gave them at Mount Sinai. After the incident of the golden calf, Yahweh tells Moses to go on to the land of Canaan, but then he delivers the bad news—he's not going with them:

> "Go up to a land flowing with milk and honey; but I will not go up *among you*, lest I consume you on the way, for you are a stiff-necked people."
>
> When the people heard this disastrous word, they mourned, and no one put on his ornaments. . . .
>
> Moses said to the LORD, "See, you say to me, 'Bring up this people,' but you have not let me know whom you will send *with me*. Yet you have said, 'I know you by name, and you have also found favor in my sight.' Now therefore, if I have found favor in your sight, please show me now your ways, that I may know you in order to find favor in your sight. Consider too that this nation is your people." And he said, "My presence will go *with you*, and I will give you rest." And he said to him, "If your presence will not go *with me*, do not bring us up from here. For how shall it be known that I have found favor in your sight, I and your people? Is it not in your going *with us*, so that we are distinct, I and your people, from every other people on the face of the earth?"
>
> And the LORD said to Moses, "This very thing that you have spoken I will do, for you have found favor in my sight, and I know you by name." (Ex 33:3-4, 12-17)

The people of Israel mourn when they hear Yahweh isn't going *with them*. Even though they are afraid of Yahweh, they still value his presence. They probably want him along mainly for protection against the Canaanites, but Yahweh's decision still affects them deeply. Yahweh informs Moses he won't go with them so that he won't consume them. This is now the second time Yahweh has distanced himself to protect his people. While it is obviously a good thing for them not to get smitten, why can't Yahweh just control himself and not destroy them? I see three reasons here.

First, he knew his people well, that they were stiff-necked, basically unwilling to be led. An ox that is "stiff-necked" does not follow the directions of the farmer. Likewise, a nation that is stiff-necked or stubborn does not obey the commands of their God (hence the golden calf), so it would need to be punished frequently. The problem isn't with the farmer but with the ox. Instead of asking the question of Yahweh, a more relevant question would be, "Why couldn't the Israelites just control themselves and do what God asked them to do?" Then there would be no problem.

Second, Yahweh wanted his people to realize that their sinful tendencies were a serious problem. Yahweh is holy, and their lack of holiness could have significant consequences. They could be destroyed or deserted by their God. Their lamenting his potential absence suggested that the message was getting through to them.

Third, he wanted them to want him. Yahweh is not like a clinging boyfriend or girlfriend who doesn't pick up the hints that the relationship is over. ("Let's just be friends.") Their behavior suggested that they didn't want him around, so he told them he was leaving. Despite their stiff-necked behavior in the past, at that point the people wept and Moses pleaded, so they apparently did want him to be present.

Now that we understand why Yahweh was saying he wouldn't go with him, we need to back up to one of the verses I skipped from the Exodus 33 section above.

Thus the LORD used to speak to Moses face to face, as a
man speaks to his friend. When Moses turned again into
the camp, his assistant Joshua the son of Nun, a young
man, would not depart from the tent. (Ex 33:11)

Even as Yahweh told his people that he was departing,
Moses and Joshua stayed close to Yahweh. Joshua never left
the tent where Yahweh's presence was meant to dwell. Joshua
had led the Israelite forces against the Amalekites (Ex 17:8-14)
and was one of only two faithful spies who were confident
that Yahweh would give them victory over the Canaanites
(Num 14:6). But perhaps the most crucial aspect of Joshua's
training to lead after the death of Moses was the time he spent
in the tent with Yahweh.

Joshua must have learned to value time with Yahweh from
his mentor, because the depth of Moses' relationship with Yahweh was unique in the Old Testament. They spoke face to face,
just like friends (Ex 33:11; Num 12:8). And Moses didn't simply
desire an intimate relationship for himself, but he wanted the
people to be close to Yahweh as well. So when Yahweh informed
Moses that he wasn't going to join them, Moses debated with
Yahweh about whether he should stay or go, and once again he
convinced God to change his mind (see chapter seven).

Although Moses' first attempt was convoluted, Yahweh still
relented and agreed to join them. However, Moses appeared not
to hear Yahweh very well (after all, he was over eighty years
old), because he repeated the initial request. So Yahweh repeated his earlier message to Moses that he had in fact changed
his mind and would go with them. I assume Moses actually did
hear it correctly the first time, but it was such a high value for
him that he wanted to double-check to be sure that Yahweh
would be going with them.

Yahweh Is with His People

God decided to remain with his people as they traveled away from Mount Sinai, but the Old Testament repeatedly informs its readers that God was with his people before and after Sinai, particularly during times of crisis. While Abraham was about to kill his beloved son Isaac, Yahweh was with him (Gen 22:11-14). While Jacob was fleeing from his homicidal brother, Yahweh was with him (Gen 28:15). While Joseph was a slave and a prisoner in Egypt, Yahweh was with him (Gen 39:2, 3, 21, 23). While Moses was a fugitive, posing as a shepherd in Midian, Yahweh was with him (Ex 3:12). While Phinehas was a gatekeeper of the tabernacle, Yahweh was with him (1 Chron 9:20). While Joshua was about to lead the Israelites in battle against the Canaanites, Yahweh was with him (Josh 1:5, 9). While Gideon was cowering in fear of the Midianites, Yahweh was with him (Judg 6:12, 16). While Samuel grew up in the evil house of Eli, Yahweh was with him (1 Sam 3:19). While Jeremiah was fearful about fighting against kings and nations, Yahweh was with him (Jer 1:8, 19).

Yahweh was with rulers of Israel and Judah: Saul (1 Sam 10:7), David (1 Sam 18:12, 14, 28), Solomon (1 Chron 29:20), Jehoshaphat (2 Chron 17:3), Ahaz (Is 7:14) and Hezekiah (2 Kings 18:7). He was with the whole nation as they went out to war (Deut 20:1), as they attempted to conquer the land (Judg 1:19, 22) and as they listened to prophetic oracles from Isaiah (41:10; 43:5), Jeremiah (42:11; 46:28) and Zechariah (8:23).

God Speaks to His People

Yeah, but what does it mean that God is with his people? The Bible says it so much it can sound like a cliché. To understand what the Old Testament means when it says God is with his people, it will be helpful to look at some specific ways God is present. He manifests his presence using extraordinary imagery involving a burning bush (Ex 3:2) and a burning pillar (Ex 13:21), an earthquake (1 Kings 19:11-12) and a whirlwind (Job 38:1; 40:6), but he appears to his people more typically in mundane ways: speaking to them, walking with them and dwelling among them.

There's a reason the Bible is called God's Word. In Scripture, God speaks to his people frequently. In the English Standard Version of the Old Testament, the phrase "The LORD said" appears more than 250 times. "Thus says the LORD" appears more than 400 times. That's a lot of divine talking. Yahweh also speaks in hundreds of other passages, without any textual marker making it explicit. The Old Testament begins with God speaking the world into creation and speaking words of blessing to the humans (Gen 1:28). The Hebrew Bible ends with Yahweh speaking through Cyrus to his entire empire, declaring that Yahweh has given him all the kingdoms of the earth and that he charged him to build him a temple, a physical manifestation of his presence, in Jerusalem (2 Chron 36:22-23).[10] English versions of the Old Testament end with Yahweh speaking through Malachi, prophesying that Elijah would come again before the day of Yahweh (Mal 4:5-6), when God himself comes to his temple (Mal 3:1-2). Along that whole way, God spoke directly to the patriarchs and later to his people through Moses, judges, kings and the prophets. He spoke through prophecies, visions, dreams (Gen 28:12; 37:5-10; Joel 2:28) and even a talking donkey (Num 22; hopefully voiced by Eddie Murphy in the animated version someday).

God Walks with His People

While people typically think of God's incarnation strictly as a New Testament idea (that is, Jesus), the Old Testament gives us numerous glimpses of God as a man. Yahweh displays human-like characteristics (anthropomorphisms) to manifest his presence to his people, sometimes taking the form of a man and walking with them, and once even wrestling with a man.

Beginning in Genesis, he made the first man out of mud and breathed into the mud-ball's mouth to give it life, then he yanked a rib out of the guy to make his spouse, and later walked through the Garden with the first couple (Gen 2:7, 21-22; 3:8). At the oaks of Mamre, Yahweh appeared to Abraham, ate a meal with him and conversed with him and his wife, Sarah (Gen 18:1-15). At Sinai, Yahweh promised to walk among the Israelites while he was their God and they his people (Lev 26:12).

Yahweh walks among his people, but he also desires that his people walk with him. Both Enoch and Noah walked with God (Gen 5:22-23; 6:9). When Abraham was ninety-nine, Yahweh commanded him to walk before him (Gen 17:1), and at the end of his life, Abraham's grandson Jacob blesses his son Joseph, describing how both Abraham and Isaac had walked before God (Gen 48:15). At Bethel, Yahweh told Jacob he would be with him as he walked to Haran to flee Esau, his brother (Gen 28:15, 20). The prophet Micah told the people that all Yahweh requires is that they do justice, love kindness and walk humbly with their God (Mic 6:8).

Jacob had a curious experience with a human incarnation of God as he was about to be reunited with his brother, Esau. When Jacob had last seen Esau, his older twin had sworn to kill him. Now Jacob's messengers had just informed him that Esau was approaching with four hundred men, so Jacob decided to cross over a stream and spend the night alone.

> And Jacob was left alone. And a man *wrestled with him* until the breaking of the day. When the man saw that he did not

prevail against Jacob, he touched his hip socket, and Jacob's hip was put out of joint as he *wrestled with him*. Then he said, "Let me go, for the day has broken." But Jacob said, "I will not let you go unless you bless me." And he said to him, "What is your name?" And he said, "Jacob." Then he said, "Your name shall no longer be called Jacob, but Israel, for you have *striven with God* and with men, and have prevailed." Then Jacob asked him, "Please tell me your name." But he said, "Why is it that you ask my name?" And there he blessed him. So Jacob called the name of the place Peniel, saying, "For I have seen God face to face, and yet my life has been delivered." The sun rose upon him as he passed Penuel, limping because of his hip. Therefore to this day the people of Israel do not eat the sinew of the thigh that is on the hip socket, because he touched the socket of Jacob's hip on the sinew of the thigh. (Gen 32:24-32)

Jacob could have written Psalm 13 as he laid down to sleep: he was afraid, he was alone, he had been cut off from his home and parents for the last twenty years, and his enemy/brother, Esau, would probably kill him the following day. Wisely, before crossing the stream, he prayed (Gen 32:7-12).

God answered his prayer in a rather unorthodox manner. While Jacob slept, God attacked him. (Maybe I won't pray tonight as I lay me down to sleep?) The two of them wrestled all night long. Wrestling matches today typically last only six or seven minutes because the sport is so grueling. Can you imagine foregoing a good eight hours of sleep before a potentially fratricidal reunion and wrestling the night away instead? The location next to a stream makes it hard to imagine that this would have been anything other than a mud-wrestling match.

Jacob's opponent seemed to be both human and divine

(sounds a bit like Jesus). He is called a man by the text; he couldn't defeat Jacob; and he had to ask Jacob his name. But he also had supernatural power to put Jacob's hip out of joint with a touch; he changed Jacob's name; and most significantly, Jacob perceived that he had wrestled with God. Jacob named the location Peniel or "Face of God," not because he had wrestled God's angel but because he had "seen God face to face." Jacob's opponent gave Jacob the name Israel or "God-wrestler," which would also suggest the opponent was divine.[11]

While I don't typically pray for a divine attacker in my sleep, God must have thought that was just what Jacob needed. Occasionally one of my sons attacks me, and we wrestle. I often regret it later, when my back goes out, but I still love wrestling with my sons. It's active, physical and close—a great way to bond with them. God apparently wanted to bond with Jacob. God took the initiative to start the match, but Jacob didn't want to let go, a bit like Moses at Sinai.

As he limped away, Jacob learned that being near God can be dangerous, but the risk is still worth it. It was good for Jacob. He came away with not just a limp but with a divine blessing and a new name. As far as we know, Jesus never wrestled with his disciples, but Yahweh had an all-night mud-wrestling match with Israel.

In many of the Old Testament passages that speak of God walking with humans or humans walking with God, a figurative meaning is clearly suggested, but in several instances, most notably with Abraham and Jacob, a physical divine presence is clearly implied. But whether a figurative or literal meaning is suggested, it is still significant that the Old Testament speaks as frequently as it does about God doing something so basic, so fundamental to human existence as walking with us.

After dinner, my wife and I often take the dog for a walk (she calls it "walking the wife"). Certain aspects of the walk involving urination, defecation and plastic bags are not the highlight of the experience, but I still love the time with Shannon and Tig. The dog loves not just being outside, relieving himself and sniffing fire hydrants (as great as those things are), but he also clearly loves just being with us. I enjoy the time with our dog, but I treasure the time with my wife. As we walk, we talk, we laugh, we tell stories. Similarly, God desires to walk with us, because walking with someone brings you closer.

God Dwells Among His People

God speaks to his people, he walks with them, and he also dwells among them. After giving instructions for the tent of meeting (also called the tabernacle) at Sinai, Yahweh declared, "I will dwell among the Israelites, and I will be their God" (Ex 29:45). While the tent of meeting worked well for Israel while they lived in tents during their wilderness wanderings, as they settled into homes in the Promised Land, David thought he should build a place for God to dwell in their midst (2 Sam 7:2). God didn't want David to build it, but he allowed David's son Solomon to accomplish the task. While the temple was being constructed, Yahweh told Solomon, "I will dwell among the children of Israel and will not forsake my people Israel" (1 Kings 6:13). Solomon's temple was dedicated about 950 B.C. (1 Kings 8).

To punish Judah for idolatry and other sins, God allowed Nebuchadnezzar of Babylon to destroy the first temple in 587 B.C. In 538 B.C., Cyrus of Persia received a commission from Yahweh to rebuild a second temple in Jerusalem (2 Chron 36:23). Eighteen years later, not much work had been done on God's house, so the word of Yahweh came to Haggai in 520 B.C., telling him to get the people moving on the rebuilding project (Hag 1).

Haggai delivered his message to the people and then something strange happened. They obeyed.

> Then Zerubbabel the son of Shealtiel, and Joshua the son of Jehozadak, the high priest, with all the remnant of the people, obeyed the voice of the LORD their God, and the words of Haggai the prophet, as the LORD their God had sent him. And the people feared the LORD. Then Haggai, the messenger of the LORD, spoke to the people with the LORD's message, "*I am with you*, declares the LORD." And the LORD stirred up the spirit of Zerubbabel the son of Shealtiel, governor of Judah, and the spirit of Joshua the son of Jehozadak, the high priest, and the spirit of all the remnant of the people. And they came and worked on the house of the LORD of hosts, their God, on the twenty-fourth day of the month, in the sixth month, in the second year of Darius the king.
>
> In the seventh month, on the twenty-first day of the month, the word of the LORD came by the hand of Haggai the prophet, "Speak now to Zerubbabel the son of Shealtiel, governor of Judah, and to Joshua the son of Jehozadak, the high priest, and to all the remnant of the people, and say, 'Who is left among you who saw this house in its former glory? How do you see it now? Is it not as nothing in your eyes? Yet now be strong, O Zerubbabel, declares the LORD. Be strong, O Joshua, son of Jehozadak, the high priest. Be strong, all you people of the land, declares the LORD. Work, for *I am with you*, declares the LORD of hosts, according to the covenant that I made with you when you came out of Egypt. My Spirit remains in your midst. Fear not.'" (Hag 1:12–2:5)

In this passage, Yahweh communicates that he is present for

his people in three ways. First, he speaks to them. Six times in nine verses the text mentions the voice of, the message of, the declaration of or the word of Yahweh. The messenger is Haggai, but the message itself clearly comes from God.

Second, the commission for his people to build Yahweh a house communicates that Yahweh wants them to have a symbolic representation of his presence nearby. Even though he allowed Solomon's temple to be destroyed, he still wants them to see a physical manifestation of Yahweh in their midst.

Third, the primary message from Yahweh via Haggai to the people is that *Yahweh is with them* already (Hag 1:13; 2:4). Interestingly, he tells them of his presence even before the temple is completed. As they obey and begin working, he is present in their midst. He also reminds them of the covenant they made at Sinai as they were coming out of Egypt, and he promises that his Spirit still remains in their midst. As they look at their humble building project and get discouraged because this second temple is "nothing" compared to Solomon's glorious structure, Yahweh wants to encourage them for their obedience and to motivate them to keep making progress. He wants them to know that he is with them.

Jesus Appeals to the Wrong Crowd

John's Gospel begins with a classic declaration about Jesus, "The Word became flesh and dwelt among us" (Jn 1:14), capturing the essence of what we've been discussing about Yahweh. Yahweh speaks; Jesus is the word. Yahweh walks; Jesus is God incarnate. Yahweh dwelt among his people; Jesus does the same. While the people of Jesus' day had a hard time comprehending his combined humanity and deity, if they read their Old Testament carefully, it shouldn't have been a shock, because Yahweh was consistently manifesting himself to his people. Yahweh was near, and now Jesus is near.

Jesus was so with the people that he scandalized religious leaders by being too close to certain people.

Now the tax collectors and sinners were all *drawing near to hear him.* And the Pharisees and the scribes grumbled, saying, "This man receives sinners and *eats with them.*"

So he told them this parable: "What man of you, having a hundred sheep, if he has lost one of them, does not leave the ninety-nine in the open country, and go after the one that is lost, until he finds it? And when he has found it, he lays it on his shoulders, **rejoicing.** And when he comes home, he calls together his friends and his neighbors, saying to them, 'Rejoice with me, for I have found my sheep that was lost.' Just so, I tell you, there will be more **joy** in heaven over one sinner who repents than over ninety-nine righteous persons who need no repentance." (Lk 15:1-7)

This passage, perhaps familiar from Sunday school, teaches profound lessons about what it meant for Jesus to be with people. Notice first that the people who drew near to Jesus were "the wrong crowd" and the religious leaders were shocked at his behavior. The tax collectors were basically traitors who extorted Jews, gave the proceeds to Rome and got rich by skimming off the top. The contemporary equivalent would be a mobster. The "sinners" here can be understood as people associated with some type of obvious immorality, which would brand them as outcasts. *Sinners* seems to be a euphemism for prostitutes since the "sinner" woman who washed Jesus' feet a few chapters earlier was probably a prostitute (Lk 7:37, 39).[12]

Why were people like this attracted to Jesus? It would be difficult to find a church today filled with mobsters and prostitutes. I see three things here that could have contributed to their attraction to him. First, Jesus told stories. He was quite a storyteller, sometimes telling parable after parable as he does in the next few chapters: the lost coin, the prodigal son, the shrewd manager, the rich man and Lazarus, the unjust judge, and the Pharisee and the tax collector. In this last parable, the tax collector, not the Pharisee, was the one who was justified (Lk 18:9-14). If I were a tax collector, I would love to hear a story that exalts a tax collector.

Second, Jesus sought after these types of people. The parable he told here makes this point powerfully. The shepherd (Jesus) left the ninety-nine sheep (the Pharisees?) and pursued the lost sheep (the tax collectors and sinners). While the religious leaders were repelled by this crowd, Jesus was drawn to them. He pursued them like he would a lost sheep, and they must have perceived his concern for them. Not surprisingly, the idea of God as shepherd pursuing lost sheep originally comes from the Old Testament, in the book of Ezekiel (Ezek 34:11-16).

Third, Jesus liked them. Just like the shepherd in the parable, Jesus liked the lost so much he threw a party when he found them. Jesus received tax collectors and sinners, ate with them and celebrated with them because he liked them, so they naturally were drawn to him. Given what Jesus was like, it's not surprising that mobsters and prostitutes were attracted to him; what is surprising is that Jesus' followers today don't generally follow his example. We are often more like the Pharisees and scribes in our aversion to and even repulsion toward the tax collectors and sinners around us.

I Had Never Picked Up a Prostitute Before

So how can followers of Jesus communicate to people that God is near? We will need to welcome and reach out to people outside the church, even those on the margins of society. Incarnating God's presence in this way will involve taking risks and putting ourselves in uncomfortable situations.

Shortly after I graduated from college, I was driving around doing errands after lunch one day. A woman was on the side of the road hitchhiking, so I picked her up. I said, "I'm Dave. What's your name?" She replied, "I'm Domino."

I thought, *That's a strange name*, but didn't pursue it. I asked about her family; she told me she didn't get along well with them, since she was "the black sheep" of the family. I naively asked, "So what makes you the black sheep?"

She was elusive, "Oh, things I've done." I was curious but decided to change subjects, "Uh, where do you work?" Her reply was unexpected, "I'm working right now." Now, I was really confused. She continued, "You could say, I'm a lady of the day-time." (It wasn't evening.)

Awkward. I finally understood. This was new to me since I had never picked up a prostitute before. I was supposed to be her "John." I told her, "Sorry to disappoint you. I won't be utilizing your services. But I'd love to pray for you." I drove her to her home, and while we sat in the car, I prayed that even though she was a "black sheep" that Jesus would find her because that's what he does. As I prayed for her, she wept. She left quickly after I was done.

I don't know what happened to Domino. The female friend of mine that I gave her phone number to was unable to reach her, but I am confident that Jesus continued to pursue her, because he loves to go after lost sheep.

EPILOGUE

Is the Answer Really "Yes, Yes and Yes"?

I was at a conference recently and told a friend that I was working on a book that asked the question "Is the God of the Old Testament angry, sexist and racist?" He replied, "Isn't the answer, 'Yes, Yes and Yes'?" (He was a New Testament professor.) As you might guess by now, I think the question deserves a slightly longer answer than that. And, not surprisingly, my answers reflect more favorably on Yahweh. And while I don't always understand him, I don't really think he behaves badly. For my expanded responses, reread the relevant chapters, but if you don't want to do that, I'll briefly summarize them now.

- Chapter one noted that Yahweh, the God of the Old Testament, has a bad reputation, and since critical perceptions of God affect readers of the Old Testament negatively, it is vital to examine these perceptions and determine if they are valid.

- Chapter two observed that Yahweh does get angry—but always legitimately so—over evil, injustice and oppression. It also pointed out that he's slow to anger and that what primarily characterizes him is love.

- Chapter three acknowledged that while Yahweh does appear sexist, he is actually highly affirming of women, making them in his image and even selecting a woman to be the spiritual and political ruler of Israel (Deborah).

- Chapter four argued that Yahweh is not racist, but is welcoming toward all nations; he even commands his people to be hospitable toward foreigners.

- Chapter five looked at the violence of Yahweh, pointing out a consistent pattern: Yahweh is willing to severely punish individuals and even nations to protect the weak and to promote peace.

- Chapter six answered the question "Is Yahweh legalistic?" with an emphatic "No" because even though we are tempted to think that God wants to burden us with laws, his commands reveal his goodness and his desire to bless.

- Chapter seven concluded that Yahweh is both stubborn and flexible: stubbornly inflexible about his commitment to bless his people, which is good news, and graciously flexible about showing mercy to repentant sinners, which is great news.

- Chapter eight observed that, even though many readers of the Bible struggle to believe that God is close, both testaments describe a God who is present—speaking to, walking with and dwelling among his people, which should be a comfort to anyone in crisis.

What Is God Like?

While I hope the review is helpful, at this point I want to emphasize that this book is essentially about the nature of God. Or to put it in a question, "What is God like?" I have focused on the God of the Old Testament because readers of the Bible struggle to understand the God they encounter in the Old Testament. People often contrast the "mean" Old Testament God with the "nice" New Testament God. But as we've looked at many biblical passages in both testaments, we've seen that Yahweh (God's name in the Old Testament) and Jesus (God's name in the New Testament) actually have a lot in common. I won't launch into an in-depth theological analysis of the Trinity (Father, Son and Holy Spirit) here, but it is important to say that Yahweh and Jesus, while they have distinct personalities, are both God and are essentially one. And most importantly, both are characterized by love.

The reason it is important to think about God's nature is that our perspective of God will determine how we relate to God. Negative images of the God of the Old Testament can have adverse effects on those of us who read the Bible. They could cause us to be embarrassed about our God, which could make us reluctant to tell nonbelievers about God. They could make us think that the Bible condones violent, sexist or racist behaviors, problems that Christians and the church have struggled with since the time of Christ. They could distance us from God (who would want to have a close relationship with an angry, sexist, racist or violent God?). They could lead us to ignore problematic texts or perhaps scare us away from reading the Bible at all.

Instead of ignoring passages that seem to portray Yahweh negatively, we need to study them, discuss them and teach them to gain understanding. While all our questions may never fully be answered, we will find that Yahweh and Jesus can be reconciled and that the God of both testaments is loving. He affirms women, is hospitable toward foreigners and brings peace, not a sword. He is not legalistic but gracious, not rigid but flexible, and not distant but near—therefore a highly attractive God.

God Is Fascinating, Relational and Good

While studying a biblical text with students, I want them to focus on the character of God, so I often ask, "What do we learn about God here?" I want them to think about what God is like based on what they read directly from Scripture, not just on what they have heard in sermons or read in books. In these chapters, we've examined many passages, and based on these passages I've used a lot of adjectives to describe what Yahweh is like (loving, affirming, hospitable, peaceful, gracious, flexible and near), but I'd like to add three more to that list. These three descriptions of God don't merely come from one chapter of this book, but in various ways appear throughout this entire book and ultimately are connected to major biblical themes throughout the entire Bible.

First, God is *fascinating*. People who think God is boring or bland need to read the Bible. God is complex. He cannot be described simply. He is both angry and loving. Even though God hates rape, he commands a woman to marry her rapist. He selects Rahab, a Canaanite prostitute, to be the ancestor of David and Jesus. He is violent, but only to punish the wicked or to protect the weak. He commands his people to have sex, to eat and to rest. He is stubborn about his promises but is flexible to forgive. He responds to Jacob's prayer by attacking him in his sleep. Since he is fascinating, we can spend the rest of our lives learning about him without being bored. Sometimes as we read the Bible we'll be confused, so we can pray for insight and ask someone about it (they probably have the same question). God is a lot of things, sometimes complex or confusing, never boring or bland, and always fascinating.

Second, God is *relational*. All of God's attributes discussed above can be understood only in the context of his relationship to his people. He loves people, affirms women, welcomes foreigners, protects the poor and forgives sinners. He speaks to, walks with and dwells among his people. He is not detached, disconnected or distant, but he takes initiative and desires to be in relationship. And since we are created in his image, we are also relational. It is literally a match made in heaven. We were designed to be in relationship with God, and that is exactly what he wants. When we wander like lost sheep, he pursues us, but there is nothing about God that should make us wander. Our lives ideally will involve a process of moving deeper into relationship with God. Just like any other relationship, depth comes from spending time together, a lot of time together. Fortunately he is just the sort of God you would want to be in relationship with, which leads to the final adjective.

Third, God is *good*. All the negative perspectives that people have about God (angry, sexist, racist and so on) can make God appear, in a word, bad. Fortunately, however, as we've looked closely at Yahweh and the Old Testament, we see a God characterized highly favorably (loving, affirming, hospitable and so on). All the positive things we've been seeing about God can also be summarized in a word, *good*. God is good. All the time. Because God is good, good things happen to bad people like us. Because he is good, his commands result in blessing for us. Because he is good, he gives us the Bible in which we learn what he is like—that he is loving, fascinating and relational.

My hope is that, as you've read this book, your picture of God has expanded. Allow that knowledge of God to shape you. Follow your fascination with God into his Word. Know that God desires relationship with you. Be assured that God is good.

In fact, God is so good that we could spend the rest of our lives declaring his goodness and thanking him for his goodness to us. I find it interesting that even though readers of the Old Testament can be troubled by what they see about God, the Old Testament is still the primary place Christians go to learn about worship and praise of God. The author of Psalm 106 understood an important truth about God, that he is good, and an important truth about us, that we were meant to praise and give thanks, so this psalm's beginning is an appropriate ending.

Praise Yahweh! Give thanks to Yahweh, for he is good, for his steadfast love [*hesed*] endures forever! (Ps 106:1)[1]

DISCUSSION QUESTIONS

Chapter One: A Bad Reputation

1. What negative images of the God of the Old Testament do you or people you know have?

2. How valid are these negative images?

3. Where do these negative images come from? The media? TV or films? The Bible?

4. What Old Testament passages do you find problematic, confusing or bizarre?

5. How is the God of the Old Testament (Yahweh) similar to, or different from, the God of the New Testament (Jesus)?

6. What do you think of Richard Dawkins's quote about Yahweh ("The God of the OT is . . . a misogynistic, homophobic, racist, infanticidal, genocidal, filicidal, pestilential, megalomanical, sadomasochistic capriciously malevolent bully")? Where do you agree or disagree with Dawkins?

7. How do negative images of Yahweh affect your desire to read, study and teach the Old Testament?

8. What can you do to better understand the God of the Old Testament?

Chapter Two: Angry or Loving?

1. Have you ever worried that God would punish you or strike you down for something you did? What was it?

2. How would you have felt if you were David and you saw Uzzah get struck down by Yahweh? What would you have said to God?

3. Have you ever ridden in the trunk of a car? Let's say you were hoping for "shotgun," how would you feel if someone asked you to ride in their trunk?

4. Tell a story about losing something important to you. How did you celebrate when you found it? How does that experience help you understand the story of the recovery of the lost ark?

5. What kinds of things make you mad? How quickly or slowly do you get angry? How difficult is it to control your temper? What do you learn about God from our own struggles to control our anger?

6. How angry do you get about a breakdown in relationship? How angry do you get about injustice or oppression?

7. When is it good to be angry? How does a person find the right balance between appropriate anger and steadfast love in relationships?

Chapter Three: Sexist or Affirming?

1. Begin the discussion by having women share any experiences of sexist comments or incidents, particularly those that occurred in the context of the church.

2. If someone were to say to you that "the Old Testament God is sexist," what would you say?

3. Which curse is worse—the man's or the woman's (Gen 3:16-19)? Why do you think so?

4. Following in the spirit of epidurals and combine harvesters, how can we work to overcome the effects of the curse, specifically the part of men ruling over women?

5. What woman from the Old Testament would you like to read about and study?

6. Why do you think Jesus praised the woman who anointed his feet so dramatically? For the men, when was the last time you, like Jesus, affirmed a woman publicly in a dramatic way?

7. End by having women share experiences of being honored or affirmed publicly by men in the context of a church.

Chapter Four: Racist or Hospitable?

1. How big of an issue is race in your culture? In the church in general? In your church specifically?

2. If God isn't racist, why does he focus so much attention on the Israelites?

3. How integrated or segregated is your church? What obstacles are there to welcoming people of other races or ethnic backgrounds?

4. What does it tell you about God that he welcomes Rahab, a Canaanite prostitute, into his people, even making her one of Jesus' ancestors?

5. What makes the story of the hospitable Samaritan such a popular story?

6. What can you do to bring up the issue of race in your church?

7. How can you be more like Saint Francis in befriending people of different races or different faiths?

8. What would the church today be like if the early Christians didn't cross ethnic barriers to spread the gospel?

Chapter Five: Violent or Peaceful?

1. How would you have felt if you were Elisha and Yahweh protected you from a gang of teens?

2. Why is the slaughter of the Canaanites so troubling? How is it similar to, or different from, modern genocides?

3. Why did the biblical authors include so much violence and warfare? Should they have edited some of that out?

4. How comfortable do you feel with the idea of violent punishment?

5. Who are your enemies? How can you love them like Elisha and Jesus did?

6. Share stories of ways you loved an enemy or someone who you didn't get along with.

7. How can you promote peace and reconciliation in your family, school, job and neighborhood?

Chapter Six: Legalistic or Gracious?

1. Why are so many Christians legalistic? How does this affect the perception of God for those outside the church?

2. Pick an Old or New Testament law that does not make sense to you (one that seems weird, bizarre, harsh or unfair). Discuss possible reasons why God would command it.

3. Pick a biblical command that is difficult to follow because it seems like God wants to deprive you of something good. How can you remind yourself that God can be trusted in this area?

4. How can you become more like the author of Psalm 119 in your love of and appreciation for God's law?

5. Which commands of God do you find easy to obey (to have sex? to eat? to rest? to feast? to help the poor?)? What is it about these commands that make them so easy to follow?

6. Why is it difficult for people in your culture to rest? When do you take a sabbath rest? What do you do on your sabbath? How do you make sure that you and your family are following God's command to rest?

Chapter Seven: Rigid or Flexible?

1. Think of a stubborn person you know (it could be you). What is it like to be around this person? When is it good that he or she is this way?

2. How easily do you change your mind? In what types of situations do you find it easy or difficult to do so?

3. How would you have felt if you were Isaiah when Yahweh told him to go back to tell Hezekiah that he had changed his mind and Hezekiah would live fifteen more years? Why would that have been difficult?

4. Do you ever feel like Jonah and wish that God wasn't merciful to someone? What types of people make you feel this way? Why?

5. Share stories of times when you were too flexible or too inflexible.

6. How do you decide when to be flexible and when to be stubborn?

Chapter Eight: Distant or Near?

1. How comfortable do you feel complaining or lamenting to God?

2. What would you have said to Jesus on the cross as he lamented?

3. Share stories of times when God seemed either distant or near during a personal crisis.

4. How does God manifest his presence to us today? How does he speak to you? When do you experience his presence?

5. What obstacles make it difficult to walk with God—like Abraham did with Yahweh or the disciples did with Jesus?

6. What do you find most appealing about Yahweh or Jesus? Why do you want to draw near to them?

7. What is the percentage of mobsters and prostitutes in your church? How can you increase that percentage to make your community more like Jesus'?

Epilogue: Is the Answer Really "Yes, Yes and Yes"?

1. What problematic Old Testament passages will you commit to read, study or teach in the future?

2. If you were truly to perceive God as fascinating, relational and good, how would that affect your life? What would you do differently?

3. What is your favorite word to describe God? Why? How can you become more like God in this respect? Pray for God's grace to help you in this process.

Notes

Chapter 1: A Bad Reputation

[1]For example, Ex 34:6; Num 14:18; Ps 86:5, 15; 103:8; 145:8; Neh 9:17; Joel 2:13; Jon 4:2.

[2]Almost three-quarters (73 percent) of the times *hell* (either *Gehenna* or *Hades*) is mentioned in the New Testament it comes from the mouth of Jesus.

[3]In the New Testament, Lot is considered "righteous" (2 Pet 2:7).

[4]We'll discuss Uzzah, Lot and the Canaanites in the following chapters.

[5]Gary Larson, *The Far Side Gallery 5* (Kansas City: Andrews McMeel, 1995), p. 40.

[6]Fortunately for both Elijah and Bruce, God was disinclined to acquiesce to their requests (he said no).

[7]"The Telltale Head," season 1, episode 8.

[8]Richard Dawkins, *The God Delusion* (New York: Mariner, 2008), p. 51.

[9]Christopher Hitchens, *God Is Not Great: How Religion Poisons Everything* (New York: Hatchette Book Group, 2007).

[10]In *The Far Side,* God also dominates as a quiz-show contestant (*Valley of The Far Side* [London: Chronicle, 1987], p. 52), cooks up a "half-baked" planet (*It Came from the Far Side* [London: Warner, 1986], p. 58) and makes snakes from clay ("Boy . . . these things are a cinch!" *The Far Side Gallery 4* [Kansas City: Andrews and McMeel, 1993], p. 18). In an episode of *The Simpsons* ("Homer the Heretic," episode 3, season 4), Homer first incurs God's wrath for skipping church, but then God is able to listen to Homer's perspective and eventually agrees.

[11]Contemporary Bible translators are apparently uncomfortable using potent words such as *smite*, but the translators of the King James Version had no such qualms.

[12]See the discussions of God's role in natural disasters in Christopher J. H. Wright's *The God I Don't Understand* (Grand Rapids: Zondervan, 2008), pp. 31-32, 44-50.

[13]*God Delusion*, p. 283. Christopher Hitchens, however, thinks the New Testament's evil exceeds that of the Old Testament (*God Is Not Great*, pp. 109-22).

[14]*Free Inquiry* 25 (2005): 9-10. See also Dawkins, *God Delusion*, p. 283.

[15]Robert Wright, "One World, Under God," *The Atlantic*, April 2009, p. 38.

[16]Tremper Longman's book *Making Sense of the Old Testament: Three Crucial Questions* (Grand Rapids: Baker, 1998) includes a helpful discussion (pp. 55-101), arguing that the biblical portrayal of God in both testaments is unified.

[17]For a more detailed discussion of divine names, see the article by David W. Baker, "God, Names of" in *Dictionary of the Old Testament: Pentateuch*, ed. T. Desmond Alex-

ander and David W. Baker (Downers Grove, Ill.: InterVarsity Press, 2003), pp. 359-68.

[18]The related form, *el*, also translated as "God," often appears in combination forms such as *el elyon*, "God Most High" (Gen 14:18), or *el shaddai*, "God Almighty" (Gen 17:1).

[19]It may seem strange to translate a personal name Yahweh, with a title, the LORD, but this pattern is simply following the Jewish tradition of saying *adonai* (LORD) instead of Yahweh when reading the Hebrew to avoid uttering the divine name.

[20]Ironically, reverence for the divine name prevents many Jews from using the name Yahweh for God.

[21]Perhaps the only situation where a title feels more intimate than a first name is in a parent-child relationship. There are only two people on the planet that can legitimately call me "Dad," and their use of that term speaks of our special and unique relationship.

[22]See Scot McKnight's excellent discussion of the command to love God and neighbor, *The Jesus Creed* (Brewster, Mass.: Paraclete Press, 2004).

Chapter 2: Angry or Loving?

[1]I apologize for the language.

[2]In his 2005 song "Indescribable," Chris Tomlin wrote that God "has told every lightning bolt where it should go." I'm not so sure.

[3]"Nuclear Materials Transportation," U.S. NRC <www.nrc.gov/materials/transportation .html> (accessed August 23, 2010).

[4]In one instance, a cart was used for people (Gen 45:19).

[5]The Old Testament never tells us what happened to the ark, but most scholars assume that it was taken (or destroyed) when Nebuchadnezzar conquered Jerusalem and sacked the temple in 587 B.C. (2 Kings 25). As we all know, it eventually was found by Indiana Jones and now rests in a U.S. government warehouse.

[6]For an excellent discussion of this text, see Walter Brueggemann, *Theology of the Old Testament: Testimony, Dispute, Advocacy* (Minneapolis: Fortress, 1997), pp. 213-28.

[7]I realize the Daytona 500 involves cars, not motorcycles.

[8]While the word "generation" (*dor*) is not included in Exodus 34:7, the context suggests it, so the New Revised Standard Version reasonably includes it

[9]Yahweh hasn't actually changed his name from Abram to Abraham yet (Gen 17:5). The tension between four hundred years of enslavement (Gen 15:13) and returning after four generations (Gen 15:16) can be easily resolved because *generation* can mean a lifetime, not only thirty years.

[10]Given what Jesus said about turning the other cheek (Mt 5:39), I assume he didn't actually strike the livestock sellers and money changers with his whip.

Chapter 3: Sexist or Affirming?

[1]Gore Vidal, quoted in Richard Dawkins, *The God Delusion* (New York: Mariner, 2008), p. 58.

[2]Voula Papas, "Women in the Bible," Atheistic Foundation of Australia <www.atheist foundation.org.au/articles/women-bible> (accessed April 23, 2010).

[3]"Proof #30: Examine God's Sexism," God Is Imaginary <http://godisimaginary.com/ i30.htm> (accessed April 23, 2010).

[4]"Is God / the Bible Sexist?" Gotquestion.org? <www.gotquestions.org/God-Bible -sexist.html> (accessed April 23, 2010).

[5]Jim Burns, "Is God Sexist?" *Christianity Today* <www.christianitytoday.com/iyf/advice/goodadvice/1.16.html> (accessed April 23, 2010).

[6]Rich Deem, "Sexism in the Bible: Is Christianity Sexist," God and Science <www.godandscience.org/apologetics/sexism.html> (accessed April 23, 2010).

[7]Amy Orr-Ewing has an excellent chapter on the topic of sexism in the Bible in *Is the Bible Intolerant?* (Downers Grove, Ill.: InterVarsity Press, 2005), pp. 85-97, but she focuses more on the New Testament than the Old Testament.

[8]For Rice, there are also other factors contributing to her decision to de-convert, see "Anne Rice: 'I Quit Christianity,'" CBS News, <www.cbsnews.com/stories/2010/07/30/entertainment/main6727348.shtml> (accessed August 18, 2010).

[9]Much of the discussion of biblical sexism centers on the Pauline epistles, but I won't discuss them here since my focus is the Old Testament.

[10]My discussion of Genesis 1–3 is profoundly shaped by many conversations over the years with my wife, Shannon.

[11]Other answers given in the class ("rib," "naked" and "mother") were either neutral or positive.

[12]While some translations render *adam* here as "man," the context requires a meaning as humans more generally, which is how many recent translations render it (TNIV, NET, NLT, NRSV). Genesis 1:27 speaks of "male and female" and verse 28 focuses on being fruitful and multiplying, which is hard to do without females.

[13]Unlike God, humans are also fallen, depraved and prone to sin.

[14]I will stay focused here on potential sexism in the Old Testament, but much has been written on Genesis 1:26-28 and how humans are meant to reflect God's image. For discussion and bibliography, see Gordon J. Wenham, *Genesis 1–15* (Waco, Tex.: Word, 1987), pp. 28-33.

[15]Brueggemann points out that since the image of God is mentioned again in Genesis 5:1 and 9:6, it means that the eating of the fruit ("The Fall") in Genesis 3 did not somehow remove the divine image from humanity. See *Theology of the Old Testament: Testimony, Dispute, Advocacy* (Minneapolis: Fortress, 1997), p. 452.

[16]For an insightful discussion of Genesis 2 and 3, see Phyllis Trible, *God and the Rhetoric of Sexuality* (Philadelphia: Fortress, 1978), pp. 72-143. She persuasively argues that the popular misogynistic readings of these texts are inaccurate interpretations.

[17]In his first epistle to Timothy, Paul isn't arguing that females are inferior to males based on Genesis 2, just that he didn't want them teaching in that particular context (1 Tim 2:13).

[18]In the one exception, false "gods" are sarcastically being called to help (Deut 32:38). William J. Webb argues that one can't argue that *ezer* suggests a superior status, but the evidence he cites suggests the opposite conclusion, and he ignores that fact that elsewhere within the Pentateuch, *ezer* is used exclusively for divine beings. *Slaves, Women & Homosexuals* (Downers Grove, Ill.: InterVarsity Press, 2001), p. 128.

[19]For example, see 1 Sam 7:12; 1 Chron 12:18; 15:26; 2 Chron 14:11; 18:31; 25:8; 26:7; 32:8; Ps 28:7; 30:10; 33:20; 37:40; 46:5; 54:4; 70:5; 79:9; 86:17; 89:19; 109:26; 115:9-11; 118:13; 121:2; 124:8; 146:5; Is 41:10, 13-14; 44:2; 49:8; 50:7, 9.

[20]Paul also states that the woman was deceived, not Adam (1 Tim 2:14).

[21]One could argue that this part of the man's curse also applies to the woman, since

both male and female corpses decay after death, but the fact remains that this part of the curse is directly targeted at the man, not the woman.

[22]I would never want to downplay the danger and pain for a woman at childbirth. At the birth of our first son, my wife lost a lot of blood. If the birth had taken place one hundred years ago, she probably would have died.

[23]See Wenham, *Genesis 1–15*, pp. 80-81; and Derek Kidner, *Genesis: An Introduction and Commentary*, Tyndale Old Testament Commentary series (Downers Grove, Ill.: InterVarsity Press, 1967), pp. 70-71.

[24]Second Peter 2:7 speaks of "righteous Lot" but never explains what this assessment is based on.

[25]A highly troubling parallel to this incident with Sodom is found in Judges 19–20, in which a brutal rape by a Benjaminite city provoked a reprisal by the remaining tribes that almost wiped out the tribe of Benjamin.

[26]David and his son Absalom both clearly thought that the rape of Tamar was wrong. While David did nothing to his oldest son, Amnon, Absalom had Amnon killed (2 Sam 13:23-29).

[27]Webb, *Slaves, Women & Homosexuals*, pp. 46-47, 76-81.

[28]See David L. Baker's discussion on this topic in *Tight Fists or Open Hands? Wealth and Poverty in Old Testament Law* (Grand Rapids: Eerdmans, 2009), pp. 16-28.

[29]Bess Twiston Davies, "Is the Bible Sexist? New Research Claims Bible's Negative Stance on Women is a Myth," The (London) *Times* Online <www.timesonline.co.uk/tol/comment/faith/article4866842.ece> (accessed April 23, 2010).

[30]References: Hannah's prayer (1 Sam 2:1-10), Mary's song (Lk 1:46-55) and Deborah's song (Judg 5:1-31). While Judges 5:1 could make it seem like Deborah and Barak wrote the song together, Deborah speaks in first person in verse 7, and in verse 12, Deborah utters the song, while Barak leads the captives.

[31]For example, the woman with the flow of blood (Mk 5:33-34), the Samaritan woman (Jn 4), the Syrophoenician woman (Mk 7:26-29) and Mary Magdalene (Jn 20:11-18).

[32]For example, the lost coin (Lk 15:8-10) and the persistent widow (Lk 18:1-8).

[33]A laborer was typically paid a denarius for a day's wage, so this would be equivalent to a laborer's annual salary.

[34]While Mark doesn't identify the individuals who rebuke her, Matthew informs us that it was the disciples (Mt 26:8).

[35]This situation is similar to a minority person bringing up the subject of race, which we will talk about in the next chapter.

Chapter 4: Racist or Hospitable?

[1]William R. Jones, *Is God a White Racist?* (Boston: Beacon Press, 1997). Jones believes that humanocentric theism is the most viable theological alternative to address the problem of racism—basically God isn't sovereign and humans have autonomy.

[2]From her album *It's Not Me, It's You.*

[3]Richard Dawkins, *The God Delusion* (New York: Mariner, 2008), p. 51.

[4]If you want to make these verses into a poster, go ahead, but use the reference: Genesis 11:12-13.

[5]Since there's no mention of God creating other humans, it appears that Seth had to marry his sister (Gen 4:26). That's worse than kissing your sister.

[6]W. H. Griffith Thomas writes, "The descendants of Ham in Africa have for centuries

been the slaves of the Japhethic races" (*Genesis: A Devotional Commentary* [Grand Rapids: Eerdmans, 1946], p. 97).

[7]William J. Webb, *Slaves, Women & Homosexuals* (Downers Grove, Ill.: InterVarsity Press, 2001), pp. 43-45, 74-76.

[8]I realize that reading these narratives in Rwanda or Sudan would make the issues more raw, as people who have been victimized by genocide would presumably have a different perspective on the violence toward the Canaanites than those of us who have been spared such horrors.

[9]See A. K. Grayson, *Assyrian Rulers of the Early First Millennium BC I (1114–859 BC)* (Toronto: University of Toronto Press, 1991), p. 201.

[10]See William W. Hallo and K. Lawson Younger, *The Context of Scripture*, vol. 2 (Leiden, U.K.: Brill, 2003), pp. 137-38.

[11]K. Lawson Younger also thinks the language of the conquest narratives is hyperbolic. *Ancient Conquest Accounts: A Study in Ancient Near Eastern and Biblical History Writing* (Sheffield, U.K.: JSOT Press, 1990), pp. 226-28.

[12]I'll discuss Israel's unsuccessful attempts at driving out the Canaanites in more detail in chapter five.

[13]It is impossible to locate precisely each of these nations, but they were all in, near or around Canaan.

[14]For the interested reader, I recommend two books by Christopher J. H. Wright that address the subject in more detail. In *Old Testament Ethics for the People of God* (Downers Grove, Ill.: InterVarsity Press, 2004), he includes an appendix discussing the issue of violence toward the Canaanites (pp. 472-80). In *The God I Don't Understand* (Grand Rapids, Zondervan, 2008), he focuses two chapters on the Canaanites (pp. 76-108).

[15]For a discussion on this topic, see Matthew Soerens and Jenny Hwang, *Welcoming the Stranger: Justice, Compassion & Truth in the Immigration Debate* (Downers Grove, Ill.: IVP Books, 2009).

[16]Yahweh also commanded them to leave behind extra grain and food in the fields for the poor and for foreigners (Lev 19:10; 23:22; Deut 24:19-21) and even to give part of their tithe to the aliens in their midst (Deut 26:12-13).

[17]*Jonah: A VeggieTales Movie, Daniel and the Lion's Den* and *Duke and the Great Pie War* (based on Ruth).

[18]See Brueggemann's insightful discussion of these two passages in his *Theology of the Old Testament: Testimony, Dispute, Advocacy* (Minneapolis: Fortress, 1997), pp. 520-22.

[19]More than twenty years ago, Ray Bakke preached one of the most memorable sermons I have ever heard, titled "Skeletons in the Closet," on the four women in Jesus' genealogy in Matthew. For a podcast of the sermon, go to <www.urbansermons .org/f/ray-bakke> (accessed August 23, 2010). For a print version, see his book, *A Theology as Big as the City* (Downers Grove, Ill.: InterVarsity Press, 1997), pp. 119-26.

[20]David Van Biema, "Can Megachurches Bridge the Racial Divide?" *Time*, January 11, 2010, pp. 38-41.

[21]It is difficult to know exactly what Francis said to the sultan almost eight hundred years ago. This quote is from Julien Green, *God's Fool: The Life and Times of Francis of Assisi* (San Francisco: Harper & Row, 1985), pp. 204-5.

Chapter 5: Violent or Peaceful?

[1]"Letter to the Editor," *The Philadelphia Inquirer,* July 2, 2009.

[2]Reginald Finley Sr., "2nd Kings 2:23—A Story of God's Love" <www.infidelguy.com/article168.html> (accessed April 23, 2010).

[3]After posting this response, I realized that *qatan* ("little") is used in conjunction with a plural form of *naar,* which can mean "boy," "lad" or "young man." *Naar,* like *yeled,* also has a wide range of meaning, as it is used to describe an adult Absalom (2 Sam 14:21). See also Donald J. Wiseman, *1 & 2 Kings,* Tyndale Old Testament Commentary (Downers Grove, Ill.: InterVarsity Press, 1993), pp. 197-98.

[4]Similarly, in courts today an individual's character is examined to help determine guilt or innocence. I recently testified as a character witness for a friend who was accused of dealing drugs (he was acquitted).

[5]For example, Mordechai Cogan and Hayim Tadmor, *II Kings: A New Translation with Introduction and Commentary* (New York: Doubleday, 1988), p. 239; and Marvin A. Sweeney, *I & II Kings: A Commentary* (Louisville, Ky.: Westminster John Knox Press, 2007), p. 419.

[6]See the discussion of Israel's laws and ancient Near Eastern parallels in Nahum M. Sarna, *Exploring Exodus: The Origins of Biblical Israel* (New York: Schocken Books, 1986), pp. 158-89.

[7]See David L. Baker, *Tight Fists or Open Hands? Wealth and Poverty in Old Testament Law* (Grand Rapids: Eerdmans, 2009), p. 207.

[8]The title of the film *Chariots of Fire* about Eric Liddell and Harold Abrahams was inspired by a William Blake poem, "Jerusalem," which alludes to "chariots of fire" that appear both in this incident and when Elijah was taken up to heaven (2 Kings 2.11).

[9]The peace appears to last for an extended period, for the next verse records that "some time later" hostilities returned (2 Kings 6:24).

Chapter 6: Legalistic or Gracious?

[1]This strip was originally published in newspapers on December 6, 1987; see also Bill Watterson, *The Authoritative Calvin and Hobbes* (Kansas City: Andrews McMeel Publishing, 1990), p. 99.

[2]However, Jesus tells the leper that he healed to offer the sacrifice Moses commanded (Mk 1:44).

[3]From "Gone, Maggie, Gone," season 20, episode 13.

[4]The infinitive absolute in this construct is typically translated as an adverb (*surely, truly, really*).

[5]For references to Satan as tempter, see Mt 4:1-11; Lk 4:1-13; 1 Cor 7:5.

[6]Harold Kushner even wrote a bestselling book on the topic, *When Bad Things Happen to Good People* (New York: Anchor, 2004).

[7]Job had bad things happen to him even though he was described as righteous (Job 1:1, 8, 22; 2:3, 10), but he was also rebuked by Yahweh (Job 38:1–40:2; 40:6–41:34) and needed to repent (Job 42:3-6).

[8]Joshua Berman, *Created Equal: How the Bible Broke with Ancient Political Thought* (New York: Oxford University Press, 2008).

[9]An untitled chart in an article by Melody Kramer, *National Geographic,* December 2009, p. 18.

[10]See Gerhard von Rad, *Deuteronomy: A Commentary* (Philadelphia: Westminster

Press, 1966), p. 141; and J. Gordon McConville, *Deuteronomy*, Apollos Old Testament Commentary (Downers Grove, Ill.: InterVarsity Press, 2002), p. 338.

[11]We discussed Mark 3:1-6 briefly in chapter two.

[12]In 2 Samuel 21, the priest's name is not Abiathar, but his father, Ahimelech. For a discussion of this problem, see the commentary of William Lane, *The Gospel of Mark* (Grand Rapids: Eerdmans, 1974), pp. 115-16.

[13]An author who has helped me think biblically about motivation for obedience is John Piper, particularly his book *Desiring God: Meditations of a Christian Hedonist* (Portland, Ore.: Multnomah, 1996).

[14]I got this paraphrase of Psalm 50 from my InterVarsity staff worker, Greg Read.

Chapter 7: Rigid or Flexible?

[1]From episode 1 ("Fun Run"), season 4.

[2]Cindy Berry (1996). Other contemporary Christian songs also describe God as unchangeable: Chris Tomlin's "Unchanging" (2002), "Indescribable" (2005) and "Unfailing Love" (2004); The David Crowder Band's "No One Like You" (2003); Vicky Beeching's "Yesterday, Today and Forever" (2006).

[3]See also the discussion on the consistency and flexibility of God in John Goldingay, *Old Testament Theology*, vol. 2, *Israel's Faith* (Downers Grove, Ill.: InterVarsity Press, 2006), pp. 88-92.

[4]While the second meaning of *regret* may imply a change of heart, and even perhaps repentance, it could simply involve sorrow or grief regarding the turn of events, so it would not necessarily suggest mutability. The third meaning involving compassion or comfort would also not necessarily infer a change on the part of the subject. Therefore, texts that use *naham* referring to divine regret (Gen 6:11; 1 Sam 15:11) or to divine compassion (Judg 2:18; Is 40:1) won't be discussed.

[5]The translators of the King James Version and the Revised Standard Version must have understood *repent* in Exodus 32:14 as simply Yahweh changing his mind about his decision to destroy Israel, so the text would not necessarily be suggesting that Yahweh is guilty of sin.

[6]Even for Saul, the consequences of his sin could have been far worse. He remains on the throne until his death in battle, recorded some fifteen chapters later (1 Sam 31).

[7]While I'm aware of the debate in theological circles regarding "open theism," this chapter does not seek to directly address the issue. I am simply making observations of biblical patterns.

[8]I feel this way often as a parent when one of my sons asks for mercy. I want to be merciful but don't want to appear too lenient.

[9]A "bucket list" includes everything you want to do right before you "kick the bucket." From the 2007 film *The Bucket List*, starring Jack Nicholson and Morgan Freeman.

[10]Although the New Revised Standard Version renders *naham* as "showed compassion," most other English versions translate the verb with a form of "relent" (ESV, RSV, NAS, NIV, TNK, NLT, NKJ).

[11]In the book of Isaiah, Yahweh poses the question, "Will I relent (*naham*) for these things?" (Is 57:6). The question initially sounds like he will not relent, but Isaiah 57:13 ends on an optimistic note, suggesting perhaps that a change was possible.

[12]Jeremiah delivers an oracle from Yahweh to the remnant still living in Judah, after the fall of Jerusalem, telling them that if they remain in the land of Judah, he will relent (*naham*) of the punishment he was bringing on them (Jer 42:10). In typical fashion, they do not believe him and not only flee to Egypt, but also kidnap Jeremiah and take him with them (Jer 43:1-7). As Jeremiah preaches in the temple, he twice exhorts the people to repent of their evil ways, so that Yahweh would then repent (*naham*) of the evil he had intended to do to them (Jer 26:3, 13). In the conclusion of this sermon, he reminds them of when Yahweh changed his mind (*naham*) about the judgment he had declared on Hezekiah after the king entreated his favor (Jer 26:19; cf. 2 Kings 20:5-6). Using the image of potter and clay, Jeremiah pronounces an oracle describing the dual nature of Yahweh's changeability in Jeremiah 18. If an evil nation turns from evil, Yahweh will relent (*naham*) concerning the evil he was going to do to them, and if a nation that Yahweh has promised to bless does evil in his sight, he will relent (*naham*) concerning the good he had intended to do for them (Jer 18:7-10).

[13]While two prophetic texts speak of Yahweh not relenting from judgment (Ezek 24:14; Zech 8:14), the immediate context of both passages reveals aspects of his merciful character. Ezekiel 24:13 describes how he had cleansed, and presumably forgiven, Jerusalem previously, yet it did not result in them remaining clean, so this time he will not forgive and relent. Zechariah describes how Yahweh had planned to bring disaster previously and did not change his mind, so in the current situation he will not change his mind about his intentions to bless Jerusalem and the house of Judah (Zech 8:15).

[14]Thomas Aquinas, *Summa Theologica*, question 9, "The Immutability of God." While I'm sure Augustine, Plato and Dionysius all have valuable things to say on this subject, I give more weight to Malachi.

[15]Richard Rice, "Biblical Support for a New Perspective," in *The Openness of God*, ed. Clark Pinnock et al. (Downers Grove, Ill.: InterVarsity Press, 1994).

[16]Ibid., p. 32.

[17]Rice later discussed Malachi 3:6 in "Biblical Support," p. 47.

[18]Jonathan Edwards, "The Most High, a Prayer-Hearing God," in *The Works of Jonathan Edwards*, vol. 2 (Carlisle, Penn.: Banner of Truth Trust, 1834), p. 115.

[19]For example, see Rice, "Biblical Support," p. 47.

[20]I realize many English translations (for example, NAS and NRSV) have Amos claiming not to be a prophet (Amos 7:14), but he also might have been simply saying that he wasn't a prophet initially (see NIV and ESV). He sure acted like a prophet, and the book with his name on it is thought to be prophetic.

[21]In the world of both the Old Testament and the New Testament, dogs weren't considered man's best friend but were viewed with contempt, as we would view rats. See, for example, Deut 23:2; 1 Sam 17:43; 2 Sam 3:8; 16:9; Phil 3:2; Rev 22:15.

Chapter 8: Distant or Near?

[1]Philip Pullman, *The Amber Spyglass* (New York: Yearling, 2000), p. 328.

[2]I've read the trilogy, and while I wouldn't consider it great fiction, Christians need not fear it. I can read Pullman or Dawkins critically, looking for points of disagreement and agreement. Christians should be able to listen to and learn from their critics.

[3]Matthew appropriately shows how this seven-hundred-year-old word of comfort to King Ahaz ("God is with us") also fits the life of Jesus. The initial context of Isaiah 7:14 is unfortunately often ignored when this passage is taught.

[4]Students often ask, "Why does God seem to approve of complaining in lament psalms but he punished Israel for it during the wilderness?" (see Ex 14:11; 15:24; 16:3; 17:3; Num 11:1, 4). In response, I make three points. First, God didn't punish the Israelites immediately for complaining in the wilderness, but he initially gave them what they asked for (food, meat, water). Second, they had just seen God dramatically deliver them from hundreds of years of enslavement, so they should have been grateful for a long time afterward. Third, they perpetually complained and never got to a place of trust and praise, which eventually made God mad.

[5]For a helpful brief discussion of laments, see Nancy L. deClaissé-Walford, *Introduction to the Psalms: A Song from Israel* (St. Louis: Chalice Press, 2004), pp. 23-25. For a deeper theological analysis of laments and their potential benefit for the church, see Walter Brueggemann, *The Psalms and the Life of Faith* (Minneapolis: Fortress, 1995), specifically the chapter "The Costly Loss of Lament," pp. 98-111.

[6]The canonization of a biblical psalm (or a book) was probably a complicated process, perhaps including multiple authors and editors, but ultimately I believe it was a divinely inspired one (2 Tim 3:16).

[7]Here is a list of forty-eight individual lament psalms: 3, 4, 5, 6, 7, 9-10, 13, 14, 17, 22, 25, 26, 27, 28, 31, 35, 38, 39, 40, 41, 42-43, 51, 52, 53, 54, 55, 56, 57, 59, 61, 64, 69, 70, 71, 77, 86, 88, 89, 102, 109, 120, 130, 139, 141, 142, 143. If that wasn't enough, here is a list of fifteen corporate laments: 12, 44, 58, 60, 74, 79, 80, 83, 85, 90, 94, 123, 126, 129, 137. I told you there were a lot.

[8]See Romans 8:38-39, Luke 1:37 and Jeremiah 29:11.

[9]Not his real name.

[10]While the English Old Testament ends with the book of Malachi, the Hebrew Bible has a different order and ends with 2 Chronicles.

[11]In Hosea 12:3-4, the text states that Jacob strove with both God and an angel.

[12]See also Craig Evans, *Luke* (Peabody, Mass.: Hendrickson, 1990), p. 123.

Epilogue

[1]Author's translation.

ACKNOWLEDGMENTS

Many people deserve thanks for their contributions to this book.

Over the course of my life, I have been taught by an impressive list of individuals. Bible teachers in InterVarsity (Paul Byer, Greg Read), at Fuller Seminary (John Goldingay, Jim Butler, Bobby Clinton), at the University of Oxford (Sue Gillingham, Hugh Williamson, Paul Joyce) have shaped my perspective not only about Scripture but also about teaching and writing.

After telling my brother Rich Lamb about my book idea in 2007, he suggested that I teach a course on the topic. During 2008 and 2009, Biblical Seminary gave me the opportunity to offer electives on the topic of the problematic behavior of God in the Old Testament, which allowed me to test ideas on helpless students (but no animals were used in the testing). While students in all of my classes have participated in a variety of ways in the book's formation, I want to specifically mention five from that first elective (Jung Kwan Youn, Sung Jin Park, Young Kim, Liz North and Jesse North), since our classroom discussions helped shape the outline of the book.

My brother Rich and his wife, Lisa, each read over chapters, providing me with valuable perspective and suggestions, as well as affirmation for my efforts. My colleagues at Biblical Seminary also read over portions and offered feedback (Steve Taylor, Todd Mangum and John Franke). Other friends read over specific chapters where I had a lot to learn and they, a lot to teach (Alison Siewert, Dakota Pippen and David Opderbeck).

When I told Scot McKnight about my topic, he immediately suggested that I contact Greg Daniel, who became my agent, and in addition to giving helpful feedback, Greg guided me through the process of finding a publisher. Al Hsu, my editor at InterVarsity Press, has given perspective on numerous aspects of the process of transforming a manuscript into a publishable book and has made the book far more readable.

My first Bible teachers were my parents, Dick and Jane Lamb. While my mother's Alzheimer's disease has prevented her from reading or even communicating much the past few years, her impact on this book is still significant as she instilled in me a deep love for God's Word from a young age. Dad has consistently supported me in many ways during my years in campus ministry and grad school. For this project his support has taken the form of interest, suggestions and encouragement.

The two arrows in my quiver (teenage sons Nathan and Noah) served as research assistants, providing me with stories and pop culture examples (I paid them $1 for each one). They make me laugh on a daily basis.

The person, however, who has shaped the writing of this book most profoundly is my wife of twenty years, Shannon. Throughout the process she listened carefully, brainstormed creatively, read graciously and, most importantly, loved consistently. She is my partner, my friend, my soul mate. It is to Shannon, therefore, that this book is dedicated.

BIBLIOGRAPHY

Baker, David L. *Tight Fists or Open Hands? Wealth and Poverty in Old Testament Law.* Grand Rapids: Eerdmans, 2009.

Bakke, Ray. *A Theology as Big as the City.* Downers Grove, Ill.: InterVarsity Press, 1997.

Berman, Joshua. *Created Equal: How the Bible Broke with Ancient Political Thought.* New York: Oxford University Press, 2008.

Brueggemann, Walter. *The Psalms and the Life of Faith.* Minneapolis: Fortress, 1995.

————. *Theology of the Old Testament: Testimony, Dispute, Advocacy.* Minneapolis: Fortress, 1997.

Cogan, Mordechai, and Hayim Tadmor. *II Kings: A New Translation with Introduction and Commentary.* New York: Doubleday, 1988.

Dawkins, Richard. *The God Delusion.* New York: Mariner, 2008.

deClaissé-Walford, Nancy L. *Introduction to the Psalms: A Song from Israel.* St. Louis: Chalice Press, 2004.

Edwards, Jonathan. "The Most High a Prayer-Hearing God." In *The Works of Jonathan Edwards.* Vol. 2. Carlisle, Penn.: Banner of Truth Trust, 1834.

Evans, Craig. *Luke.* Peabody, Mass.: Hendrickson, 1990.

Goldingay, John. *Old Testament Theology, vol. 2: Israel's Faith.* Downers Grove, Ill.: InterVarsity Press, 2006.

Grayson, A. K. *Assyrian Rulers of the Early First Millennium BC I (1114-859 BC).* Toronto: University of Toronto Press, 1991.

Griffith Thomas, W. H. *Genesis: A Devotional Commentary.* Grand Rapids: Eerdmans, 1946.

Hallo, William W., and K. Lawson Younger. *The Context of Scripture.* Vol. 2. Leiden, U.K.: Brill, 2003.

Hitchens, Christopher. *God Is Not Great: How Religion Poisons Everything.* New York: Hatchette, 2007.

Jones, William R. *Is God a White Racist?* Boston: Beacon Press, 1997.

Kushner, Harold. *When Bad Things Happen to Good People.* New York: Anchor, 2004.

Longman, Tremper, III. *Making Sense of the Old Testament: Three Crucial Questions.* Grand Rapids: Baker, 1998.

McConville, J. G. *Deuteronomy.* Downers Grove, Ill.: InterVarsity Press, 2002.

Mortenson, Greg, and David Oliver Relin. *Three Cups of Tea: One Man's Mission to Promote Peace . . . One School at a Time.* New York: Penguin Books, 2007.

Orr-Ewing, Amy. *Is the Bible Intolerant?* Downers Grove, Ill.: InterVarsity Press, 2005.

Piper, John. *Desiring God: Meditations of a Christian Hedonist.* Portland, Ore.: Multnomah, 1996.

Rad, Gerhard von. *Deuteronomy: A Commentary.* Philadelphia: Westminster Press, 1966.

Rice, Richard. "Biblical Support for a New Perspective." In *The Openness of God,* ed Clark Pinnock et al. Downers Grove, Ill.: InterVarsity Press, 1994.

Sarna, Nahum M. *Exploring Exodus: The Origins of Biblical Israel.* New York: Schocken Books, 1986.

Seibert, Eric A. *Disturbing Divine Behavior: Troubling Old Testament Images of God.* Minneapolis: Fortress, 2009.

Soerens, Matthew, and Jenny Hwang. *Welcoming the Stranger: Justice, Compassion & Truth in the Immigration Debate.* Downers Grove, Ill.: IVP Books, 2009.

Sweeney, Marvin A. *I & II Kings: A Commentary.* Louisville, Ky.: Westminster John Knox Press, 2007.

Trible, Phyllis. *God and the Rhetoric of Sexuality.* Philadelphia: Fortress Press, 1978.

Webb, William J. *Slaves, Women & Homosexuals: Exploring the Hermeneutics of Cultural Analysis.* Downers Grove, Ill.: InterVarsity Press, 2001.

Wenham, Gordon J. *Genesis 1-15.* Waco, Tex.: Word, 1987.

Wiseman, Donald J. *1 & 2 Kings.* Tyndale Old Testament Commentary. Downers Grove, Ill.: InterVarsity Press, 1993.

Wright, Christopher J. H. *Old Testament Ethics for the People of God.* Downers Grove, Ill.: InterVarsity Press, 2004.

Wright, Christopher J. H. *The God I Don't Understand.* Grand Rapids: Zondervan, 2008.

Younger, K. Lawson. *Ancient Conquest Accounts: A Study in Ancient Near Eastern and Biblical History Writing.* Sheffield, U.K.: JSOT Press, 1990.

Scripture Index